# Rewire Me

*Don't Conform But Be Transformed*

Naomi Greenlee

**Naomi Greenlee**
**Rewire Me**



Published by Spines

ISBN: 979-8-89691-265-1

2025

# REWIRE ME

Combines science, faith, and mind renewal to help readers overcome negativity and transform lives.

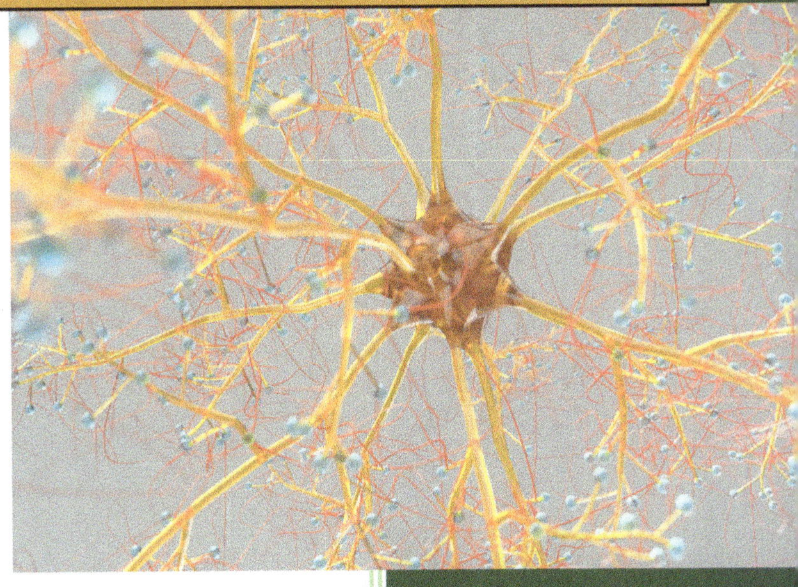

## Naomi Greenlee

Combines science, faith, and mind renewal to help readers overcome negativity and transform lives.

1/1/2025

The contents of REWIRE ME draw from over 15 years of studying videos of neuroscience, personal experiences, and bible principles. Insights from leading neuroscientists, practical applications, and scriptural truths combine to empower transformative mind renewal.

# Rewire Me

# Contents

# Preface

We live in a world that constantly shapes our thoughts, behaviors, and beliefs. Every day, we encounter experiences – good or bad – that form the wiring of our minds. But what if I told you that we have the power to rewire those patterns? What if our minds, through conscious effort and divine guidance, can be transformed to align with truth, purpose, and wholeness?

In this journey, I invite you to explore the concept of rewiring your mind. Drawing from cutting-edge neuroscience and wisdom found in God-ordained scripture, we'll uncover how the brain and the mind are not the same. Dr. Caroline Leaf, a renowned neuroscientist and believer, reminds us that while the brain is a physical organ, the mind is the driving force that influences and shapes it. It's through our mind- how we think, perceive, and choose – that we can actively transform our brains and, ultimately, our lives. Knowing that science and the Bible have the same author, GOD, should free us to follow Him intently, knowing that truth originates and ends with Him. Whenever science differs from God's Word, scripture takes precedence over science, and science will eventually catch up.

Over the past 15 years, my studies of the brain, mind, science, and scripture have shown me something profound: science and the Bible agree far more than they disagree. While many view these fields as being at odds, I believe science is merely catching up to what Scripture has already revealed for thousands of years. Science is now proving what verses like "As a man thinketh in his heart, so is he" (Proverbs 23:7) have long declared -our thoughts shape who we are and the lives we lead. This convergence of truth, both scientific and spiritual, offers us a clear roadmap for transformation.

Romans 12:2 tells us, "Do not conform to the pattern of this world, but be transformed by the renewing of your mind." This call to transformation is not a passive suggestion but an invitation to engage in a process of intentional rewiring. Science now affirms what scripture has already revealed: our thoughts are powerful. They create pathways in our brain, much like trails through a forest, determining the way we navigate life.

In the following chapters, we'll discuss practical steps to identify and change unhealthy thought patterns, cultivate new habits, and renew your perspective with God's Word as your guide. You'll learn to distinguish between your mind and your brain, understanding that the mind, the nonphysical essence of your thinking, choosing, and feeling holds the key to reshaping your reality.

If you're ready to change the way you think, feel, and live, this book is for you. Let's take this journey together, step by step, toward a renewed mind and a transformed life. It's time to **REWIRE ME**.

# Chapter One

## Scripture as the Ultimate Authority: Science Affirming God's Truths"

*"The heavens declare the glory of God; the skies proclaim the work of his hands. Day after day they pour forth speech; night after night they reveal knowledge." (Psalm 19:1-2)*

In the beginning, God created the heavens and the earth, as declared in Genesis 1:1, and this profound act of creation aligns with the wonder revealed through science. The vast universe, intricately ordered with galaxies, stars, and planets, speaks to an intelligent Designer who fine-tuned the laws of physics to sustain life. Science reveals that the universe had a definite beginning, a moment of origin often referred to as the Big Bang, echoing the scriptural assertion of creation ex nihilo (out of nothing). The balance of ecosystems, the complexity of DNA, and the precise conditions that allow life on Earth point to a Creator whose handiwork is evident in all things. Together, scripture and science invite us to marvel at a God whose power and wisdom are woven into the fabric of creation.

The Bible is the ultimate authority because it is the inspired Word of God, offering timeless truths that guide us in every area of life.

Scripture addresses the origin of life, the purpose of humanity, moral standards, and the path to salvation. Its teachings remain relevant across generations, providing a foundation for truth and wisdom. In 2 Timothy 3:16, we read, "All Scripture is God-breathed and is useful for teaching, rebuking, correcting, and training in righteousness." This verse highlights the Bible's role as the standard by which we measure truth.

Science, on the other hand, offers a systematic approach to understanding the natural world, giving us additional insights into the intricacies of God's creation. As scientific discoveries advance, they often affirm what scripture has already revealed. For example, the Bible described the earth as round (Isaiah 40:22) says, "He sits enthroned above the circle of the earth, and its people are like grasshoppers", and suspended in space (Job 26:7) says, "He spreads out the northern skies over empty space; he suspends the earth over nothing", long before these concepts were understood scientifically. Similarly, modern studies on mental health align with biblical teachings on the power of gratitude, rest, and positive thinking.Science, on the other hand, offers a systematic approach to understanding the natural world, giving us additional insights into the intricacies of God's creation.

While science evolves and catches up to truths revealed in scripture, it serves as a valuable tool for exploring God's creation. Together, they provide a comprehensive understanding of life, with scripture offering divine wisdom and science providing additional details about God's handiwork.

The relationship between scripture and science has long been a subject of fascination and debate. For believers, the Bible is the ultimate authority, a divine revelation of God's truth that provides guidance on spiritual, moral, and even practical matters. Science on the other hand, is a tool for understanding the natural world, uncovering the laws and principles that govern creation. While some see scripture and science as opposing forces, a closer look reveals that they are complementary. Science often confirms what scripture has long proclaimed, showing how both can work together to deepen our understanding of truth.

## The Authority of Scripture

The Bible is not merely a collection of ancient texts; it is the inspired Word of God, revealing eternal truths that transcend time and culture. It provides answers to life's most profound questions: Who are we? Why are we here? What is our purpose? From Genesis to Revelation, scripture paints a cohesive picture of God's plan for humanity.

One of the key reasons the Bible is the ultimate authority is its divine authorship. In 2 Timothy 3:16, we read, "All scripture is God-breathed and is useful for teaching, rebuking correcting, and training in righteousness." This verse establishes the Bible as more than just a historical or moral document, it is divinely inspired, carrying the authority of God Himself. As such, its teachings are not subject to human opinion or revision; they stand as absolute truth.

Additionally, the Bible's consistency across 66 books, written by over 40 authors over a span of approximately 1,500 years, is unparalleled. Despite the diversity of its authors and the times in which they lived, the Bible maintains a unified message. This coherence underscores its divine origin and reinforces its authority.

Scripture also provides a moral framework that has shaped civilizations for millennia. Its principles of justice, love, joy, humility, and forgiveness remain foundational to human ethics. Unlike human philosophies, which shift with societal trends, the Bible's teachings are unchanging. Isaiah 40:8 reminds us, "The grass withers, the flower fades, but the word of our God will stand forever."

## The Role of Science

While scripture provides spiritual and moral truths, science offers a systematic way to study and understand the physical world. Through observation, experimentation, and reasoning, science uncovers the intricate details of God's creation. It helps us understand natural phenomena, from the vastness of the cosmos to the complexity of the human body, namely the brain in this book.

Science, however, is not the ultimate authority. It is a human endeavor, limited by our understanding and constantly evolving. Theories once considered groundbreaking are often revised or replaced as new evidence emerges. Despite its limitations, science is a valuable tool that allows us to marvel at the complexity and order of God's creation.

The Bible encourages the pursuit of knowledge and understanding. Proverbs 25:2 states, "It is the glory of God to conceal a matter; to search out a matter is the glory of kings." This verse highlights the idea that exploring the mysteries of the universe is an act of worship, a way to honor God by appreciating the work of His hands.

## Scripture's Alignment with Scientific Discoveries

Although the Bible is not a scientific textbook, it contains numerous statements that align with modern scientific understanding, often centuries or even millennia before science made the same discoveries. These examples demonstrate that scripture and science are not at odds but can complement one another.

## 1. The Earth's Shape and Position

Long before the advent of modern astronomy, the Bible described the earth in ways that align with scientific discoveries. Isaiah 40:22 says, "He sits enthroned about the circle of the earth," indicating a spherical earth rather than a flat one. Additionally, Job 26:7 states, "He spreads out the norther skies over empty space; he suspends the earth over nothing." These descriptions predate scientific confirmations of the earth's shape and its suspension in space by thousands of years.

## 2. The Hydrological Cycle

The Bible accurately describes the water cycle, a concept not fully understood until the 16th and 17th centuries. Ecclesiastes 1:7 observes, "All streams flow into the sea, yet the sea is never full. To the place the streams come from, there they return again." Similarly, Job 36:27-28 explains, "He draws up the drops of water, which distill as rain to the streams; the clouds pour down their moisture and abundant showers fall on mankind."These verses reflect a sophisticated understanding of evaporation, condensation, and precipitation.

## 3. Human Physiology and Hygiene

Biblical instructions regarding hygiene and quarantine, such as those found in Leviticus, reveal an understanding of disease prevention that was far ahead of its time. For instance, Leviticus 13:4-5 describes isolating individuals with infectious skin diseases to prevent the spread of illness, a practice that aligns with modern principles of quarantine. Similarly, the emphasis on washing with water (Leviticus 15:13) aligns with modern sanitation practices.

## 4. The Expanding Universe

Modern cosmology has revealed that the universe is expanding, a discovery attributed to Edwin Hubble in the 20th century. However, the Bible alludes to this concept in verses like Isaiah

40:22, which describes God as one "who stretches out the heavens like a canopy, and spreads them out like a canopy, and spreads them out like a tent to live in." This imagery suggests an expanding universe long before it became a scientific consensus.

## Science Catching Up to Biblical Wisdom

While science often affirms biblical truths, it is important to recognize that scripture operates on a higher plane of understanding. The Bible reveals truths about human nature, morality, and the spiritual realm that science cannot measure or quantify. However, as scientific methods and tools improve, they increasingly align with what scripture has long declared.

For example, The Bible emphasizes the power of gratitude and positive thinking. Philippians 4:8 encourages believers to focus on what is true, noble, and praiseworthy. Modern psychology and neuroscience now confirm that practices like gratitude journaling and positive affirmations can rewire the brain, reduce stress, and improve mental health.

Another area where science is catching up is the importance of rest. The Bible established the principle of the Sabbath in Genesis 2:2-3, emphasizing the need for regular rest and restoration. Today, medical research highlights the importance of rest for physical and mental health, showing that adequate sleep and work-life balance are essential for well-being.

# The Complementary Relationship Between Scripture and Science

Rather than viewing scripture and science as competing forces, we should recognize their complementary nature. Scripture provides the "why," offering purpose and meaning, while science explores the "how," uncovering the mechanisms of God's creation. Together, they form a comprehensive framework for understanding life and the universe.

For believers, this integration deepens faith and fosters awe for God's wisdom and power. Psalm 19:1 declares, "The heavens declare the glory of God; the skies proclaim the work of his hands." Scientific discoveries about the vastness of the universe, the complexity of DNA, or the precision of natural laws serve as reminder of God's magnificence.

The Bible stands as the ultimate authority, offering divine truths that guide us in every area of life. Science, though limited and ever-evolving, provides valuable insights that often affirm and complement scripture and science work together to reveal the brilliance of God's creation and the timeless wisdom of His Word.

As science continues to advance, it uncovers more evidence of the truths the Bible has proclaimed for millennia. This harmony between scripture and science reminds us that all truth is God's truth. By embracing both, we can live lives that are not only grounded in faith but also enriched by understanding, glorifying God in all that we do.

**"Scripture is the blueprint of truth, and science is the discovery of God's design; together, they reveal the harmony of faith and understanding."**

— Naomi

## CLOSING PRAYER

Heavenly Father,

We come before You in awe of Your wisdom and power, recognizing that all truth comes from You. Thank You for the gift of Your Word, which provides us with the ultimate foundation for our lives. Your scripture is a lamp to our feet and a light to our path, guiding us through every season and challenge.

Lord, we also thank You for the tools of science that allow us to marvel at the intricacy and beauty of Your creation. You have given us minds to explore, discover, and understand the world You spoke into existence. Help us to see how science affirms and complements the external truths of Your Word, drawing us closer to You as we uncover the mysteries of Your handiwork.

Father, give us discernment to recognize Your truth amidst the noise of the world. Strengthen our faith to trust in Your Word as the ultimate authority and to use the knowledge we gain thorough science to glorify You. May our hearts remain humble, our minds open and our spirits aligned with Your will.

We pray that You continue to reveal Your truth to us, deepening our understanding and equipping us to live lives that reflect Your glory. In all we do, may we honor You as the Creator, Sustainer, and ultimate source of wisdom.

In Jesus' name, we pray. Amen.

# Chapter Two

## The Power of the Mind

*"For as he thinks in his heart, so is he." (Proverbs 23:7)*

Our thoughts have power- far more than most of us realize. Every thought we think sends signals throughout our brain, creating and strengthening neural pathways. If we were to compare it to a garden, our mind plants seed of thoughts that either grow into flourishing life giving plants or choking weeds.

Dr. Caroline Leaf describes the brain as the hardware of a computer, while the mind acts as the software. Your mind determines the instructions your brain will follow. The mind directs how you process experiences, respond to emotions, and make decisions. This distinction is profound because it gives us control. You are not a victim of your brain. You are the driver of your mind.

The Bible tells us repeatedly that we must guard our thoughts. Philippians 4:8 instructs us to think on these things that are "true, noble, right, pure, lovely, and admirable." Why? Because our thoughts have the power to build or destroy our lives. Thoughts of fear, doubt, and bitterness can trap us in destructive cycles, while thoughts of faith, hope, and love can rewire us to live fully and freely.

Neuroscience now confirms that our brains are not fixed but neuro-plastic -they can be changed. Every time you choose a new thought, you create new neural connections. Over time, these connections become stronger, while old pathways of toxic thinking weaken. This is where the power of rewiring comes in. By intentionally choosing what you think, you are reshaping your brain's structure. As powerful as the mind is, it cannot have two thoughts at the same time, so you get to choose which thought you will dwell on that comes to your mind or that you bring to your mind.

Here's the good news, you are not powerless. By understanding this connection between your mind, brain, and scripture, you can begin the process of rewiring. This process is not an instant fix, nor is it something you do once and forget. It's a journey, an intentional prac-tice of aligning your thoughts with God's Word and reshaping the patterns in your brain that have been established over time. It's not always easy, but with commitment and God's help, transformation is possible. Through the life and teachings of my Lord and Savior Jesus Christ, we see the ultimate example of resilience, as He endured trials, overcame adversity, and provided a path for us to walk in freedom and victory.

When Paul wrote in Romans 12:2, "Do not conform to the pattern of this world, but be transformed by the renewing of your mind,"he was highlighting a profound truth that science now confirms: your mind can change, and so can your brain. For years, it was believed that the brain was a fixed organ, unchanging after a certain age. However, modern neuroscience reveals that the brain is neuroplastic, meaning it can adapt, reorganize, and even grow new neural pathways. This is powerful news for anyone feeling trapped in cycles of fear, doubt, or negative thinking.

What does this look like in practice? It begins with awareness, being mindful of the thoughts that dominate your mind. Scripture repeatedly calls us to "take every thought captive to make it obedient to Christ" (2 Corinthians 10:5). This means identifying the lies you may have unknowingly believed: I'm not good enough," "I'll never succeed," or "God doesn't care about me." These thoughts repeated over time, form neural pathways in the brain that dictate your responses and emotions. But here's where the transformation begins: when you replace these lies with God's truth, you start building new pathways.

For example, if you lived under the lie of inadequacy, you could counter it with verses like Philippians 4:13: "I can do all things through Christ who strengthens me." As you meditate on this truth and declare it daily, your brain starts to form new connections. The more you repeat it, the stronger these connections become, eventually replacing the old patterns. This isn't just spiritual encouragement; it's a scientifically supported process. Neuroscientists call this, "synaptic pruning," where unused pathways weaken and die off while frequently used ones strengthen.

Prayer and meditation on God's Word also play a vital role in this rewiring process. Studies show that intentional prayer reduces stress, increases focus, and changes the structure of the brain in ways that promote peace and resilience. When you bring your worries and struggles to God, you're not only finding spiritual strength but also rewiring your brain to respond to challenges with faith instead of fear.

Journaling is another practical tool for this transformation. Writing down your thoughts, prayers, and scriptures you're standing on helps solidify these truths in your mind. Journaling allows you to reflect on the changes you're seeing over time, which reinforces the new pathways you're building.

Finally, community is key. Surrounding yourself with like-minded believers provides encouragement, accountability, and examples of others who have walked this journey of renewal. Proverbs 27:17 says, "As iron sharpens iron, so one person sharpens another."The right relationships can help you stay grounded in truth and remind you of God's promises when you're struggling to see them yourself.

The process of rewiring your mind is not about self-reliance; it's about partnering with God. As you align your thoughts with His Word and trust in His power, you'll begin to see changes not only in your mindset but in every area of your life. Patterns of fear can be replaced with confidence. Cycles of negativity can give way to hope. And strongholds that once seemed impossible to overcome will crumble under the truth of God's promises.

You have the tools, and you have the power through Christ. Transformation is possible, and it starts with one step: choosing to believe that change can happen and taking action to make it a reality. Your mind is not your enemy, it's your greatest ally when renewed by God's truth. So, embrace the journey, trust the process, and watch as God works in you and through you to bring about lasting transformation.

Let's start by identifying your dominant thought patterns. Are they aligned with truth? Or are they rooted in fear, negativity, or lies? In the next section, we'll discuss how to recognize and replace toxic thoughts with life-giving ones.

# Breaking Free from Toxic Thought Patterns

Our lives are shaped by the thoughts we allow to dominate our minds. Toxic thought patterns like fear, self-doubt, bitterness, or negativity, become strongholds that keep us trapped in cycles of defeat and limitation. Often, we don't even realize how deeply these patterns are ingrained. The mind becomes conditioned to follow familiar routes, no matter how destructive they may be.

Dr. Caroline Leaf explains that every thought creates a physical change in the brain, forming neural pathways. Repeated toxic thoughts create "trenches," like deep grooves, that become the default responses to life's challenges. However, just as negative thoughts can build unhealthy patterns, intentional, positive, and truthful thoughts can help us build new, life-giving pathways.

Scripture highlights this principle in 2 Corinthians 10:5: "We take captive every thought to make it obedient to Christ." This verse is a call to action. It reminds us that we can break free from toxic thinking by identifying those thoughts, rejecting their influence, and replacing them with God's truth.

To start, ask yourself:

- What are the recurring thoughts that dominate my mind?
- Are they building me up or tearing me down?
- Do they align with God's promises or contradict His Word?

Toxic thoughts don't disappear on their own. They must be actively uprooted and replaced. In the next section, we'll explore practical strategies to interrupt negative patterns and create new ones that align with truth, health, and purpose.

Breaking free from toxic thoughts is not a one-time event; it requires sustained effort and discipline. Toxic thoughts often attempt to resurface, especially during times of stress and doubt. That's why maintaining freedom involves consistent spiritual and practical practices.

Science also confirms that mindfulness and intentional focus can sustain mental clarity and emotional well-being. By regularly pausing to reflect, pray, and reset your thoughts, you create a habit of redirecting your mind away from negativity.

Remember to celebrate progress. Every step toward freedom is a victory. Acknowledge how far you've come and thank God for His guidance. By cultivating gratitude and focusing on growth, you reinforce positive thought patterns and break the cycle of toxic thinking for good.

When it comes to breaking free from toxic thought patterns, celebrating progress is not just an optional practice, it's essential for lasting change. Toxic thinking thrives in an environment of shame, self-criticism, and negativity. It tells you that unless you've achieved perfection, you've failed. But the truth is, growth is a process, and even the smallest victories are evidence of God working in your life. Celebrating these victories shifts your focus from what's lacking to what's possible, helping you see the progress you've made and the faithfulness of God in guiding you forward.

Gratitude is a powerful weapon in this fight. Toxic thoughts are often rooted in scarcity, the belief that you're not enough, that there isn't enough time, resources, or hope to overcome your struggles. Gratitude interrupts this narrative by redirecting your attention to what you do have and what God has already done. When you take time to thank Him for the small wins, like a moment of peace in the middle of a busy day or the strength to say no to a harmful habit, you're retraining your brain to look for the good instead of dwelling on the bad. Over time, this shift in focus creates a mental environment where toxic thoughts struggle to take root.

Another important aspect of breaking free is learning to reframe setbacks. Toxic thinking tells you that any failure is proof you're not good enough. But in God's hands, even our mistakes can become tools for growth. When you fall back into an old thought pattern, instead of spiraling into self-criticism, take it as an opportunity to learn. Ask yourself: What triggered this thought? What truth can I replace it with next time? By approaching setbacks with curiosity instead of condemnation, you weaken the power of toxic thinking and strengthen your ability to respond with grace and wisdom.

In this process, it's also important to surround yourself with positive influences. Toxic thoughts are often reinforced by negative environments, whether it's the media you consume, the people you spend time with, or even the self-talk you engage in daily. Evaluate these influences honestly. Are they helping you grow or pulling you back into old patterns? Seek out relationships and resources that encourage and uplift you. Spend time in God's Word, which is the ultimate source of truth and renewal. Verses like Philippians 4:8 remind us to focus on what is true, noble, right, pure, lovely, admirable, excellent, or praiseworthy. As you fill your mind with these things, toxic patterns lose their grip.

One of the most powerful tools in breaking free is forgiveness, both for yourself and for others. Toxic thoughts often stem from unresolved hurts, whether it's bitterness toward someone who wronged you or shame over your own past mistakes. Holding on to these hurts only reinforces the cycle of negativity. Forgiveness doesn't mean minimizing the pain you've experienced, but it does mean releasing it to God and trusting Him to bring justice and healing. When you forgive, you free yourself from weight of toxic emotions and create space for God's peace to fill your heart and mind. Science shows that forgiveness reduces stress, improves mental health, and lowers blood pressure.

Ephesians 4:32, "Be kind and compassionate, forgiving each other, just as in Christ forgave you."

Finally, don't underestimate the power of consistency. Breaking free from toxic thought patterns is not a one-time event; it's a daily commitment. Every time you choose gratitude over negativity, truth over lies, and hope over despair, you're reinforcing new pathways in your brain. These small, consistent choices add up over time, leading to lasting transformation. Celebrate each moment you catch yourself thinking differently, and trust that God is working in you to renew your mind day by day.

Freedom from toxic thoughts is not about achieving perfection, it's about progress and perseverance. As you cultivate gratitude, reframe setbacks, and surround yourself with positive influences, practice forgiveness, and stay consistent, you'll find that the chains of toxic thinking grow weaker and weaker. Step by step, you're moving closer to the freedom God has promised you, a life of peace, joy and a mind fully aligned with His truth.

## The Power of Awareness: Identifying Toxic Thought Patterns

Initially, you must recognize the battle in your mind. The first step to breaking free from toxic thought patterns is recognizing the battlefield, the mind. The bible clearly identifies the mind as a critical area of spiritual and emotional warfare. In 2 Corinthians 10:4-5, Paul writes, "The weapons we fight with are not weapons of the world. On the contrary, they have divine power to demolish strongholds. We demolish arguments and every pretension that sets itself up against the knowledge of God, and we take captive every thought to make it obedient to Christ."

Toxic thoughts often disguise themselves as harmless worries, doubts, or self-criticisms. Over time, these thoughts grow into strongholds, deeply rooted patterns that influence how we perceive ourselves, others, and even God. For example, thoughts like "I'm not good enough" or "I'll never succeed" might seem minor, but they shape actions and decisions. Recognizing these patterns is vital because you cannot change what you refuse to confront.

Science supports this biblical truth. Cognitive-behavioral studies show that thoughts directly influence emotions and behaviors. By identifying recurring negative thoughts, you can begin the process of breaking free. Start by journaling your thoughts or praying for discernment to uncover hidden toxic beliefs. Awareness is the foundation for transformation.

## Practical Strategies to Interrupt Toxic Thoughts

### 1. Identify and Write Down Toxic Thoughts

- Take Time to reflect on recurring thoughts that dominate your mind. Write them down in a journal or notebook. For example:
    - "I'm not good enough."
    - "Nothing will ever change."
    - "I'll always fail."
- Writing these thoughts out brings them into the light, helping you recognize their influence over your life.

### 2. Challenge the Lies with Truth:

- Compare each toxic thought with scripture and truth. For example:

- **Toxic thought:**"I'm not good enough."
- **Truth:**"I am fearfully and wonderfully made." (Psalm 139:14)
- **Toxic thought:**"Nothing will ever change."
- **Truth:**"With God, all things are possible." (Matthew 19:26)
- **Toxic thought:**"I'll always fail."
- **Truth:**"I can do all things through Christ who strengthens me." (Philippians 4:13)
- **Toxic thought:**"I know God is able, but I don't think He wants to do it for me."
- **Truth:**"I would that you would prosper and be in health even as your soul prospers." (3 John 1:2) (This states that God wants you to be successful, He wants you to be healthy as your mind, will, and emotions prospers)

Write the truth next to each toxic thought. Repeat these truths daily as affirmations to rewire your thinking.

### 3. Replace the Toxic Thought Immediately:

- When a toxic thought arises, don't dwell on it. Take it captive by immediately replacing it with a positive, truthful thought. For instance.
- **Toxic thought:**"I can't handle this."
- **Replacement:**"God gives me the strength to handle all things."
- By consistently interrupting toxic thoughts, you weaken their power and begin to form healthier patterns

### 4. Speak Life Over Yourself

- Words have power. Speak out God's promises over your life daily. "Death and life are in the power of the tongue." (Proverbs 18:21)

For example:

- I am strong, capable, and loved by God."
- God has a plan for my life, and it is good."

Verbal affirmations help solidify new thought patterns, reinforcing the truth in your mind.

**5. Practice Gratitude Daily:**

- Gratitude helps shift your focus from negativity to what is good. Each day, write down three things you're grateful for, no matter how small. Gratitude rewires your brain to notice blessings instead of problems.

## Scriptural Encouragement

The process of renewing your mind doesn't happen overnight, but God promises transformation when we persist. Romans 12:2 reminds us: "Do not conform to the pattern of this world but be transformed by the renewing of your mind."

This transformation is not just spiritual, it is also neurological. Each time you reject a toxic thought and replace it with God's truth, you are reshaping your brain. This is the power of neuroplasticity, the brain's ability to form new connections based on how we think. Science is now affirming what the Bible declared long ago: we are not slaves to our thoughts. Through God's Word, we can renew our minds and walk in freedom.

Memorize and meditate on scripture to reinforce truth in your mind. Additionally, gratitude, journaling, and speaking God's promises aloud. Over time, these practices shift your thought patterns, aligning them with God's truth.

## Reflection Exercise

Take a moment to answer these questions in your journal:

1.  What are three recurring toxic thoughts you've struggled with?
2.  Which scriptures or truths can replace these thoughts? Write them down.
3.  How will you remind yourself to replace these thoughts the next time they arise?

As you commit to the process, remember that transformation is a journey. Be patient with yourself, and trust that with God's help, you can break free from toxic thought patterns and create a mind aligned with His truth.

**"The mind holds the power to break free from the chains of toxic thoughts; awareness is the key, and transformation begins with what you choose to see."**

— Naomi

## Closing Prayer

Heavenly Father,

Thank You for the gift of my mind and the power You've given me to choose my thoughts. I confess that I have allowed toxic thinking to take root in my life, but today, I surrender my thoughts to You. Help me to take every thought captive and make it obedient to Your truth.

Lord, renew my mind with Your Word. When fear, doubt, or negativity try to overwhelm me, remind me of Your promises. Give me the strength to reject lies and replace them with thoughts that reflect Your love, grace, and purpose for my life.

I invite You Holy Spirit to guide me as I walk this journey of transformation. Teach me to see myself and my circumstances through Your eyes. I believe that with Your help, I can rewire my mind and live in the freedom and victory You have promised.

In Jesus' name, Amen.

# Chapter Three

## The Mind, The Brain, and The Spirit

"Set your mind on things above, not on earthly things." (Colossians 3:2)

To rewire our minds, we must first understand the difference between the mind and the brain, a concept often overlooked, yet foundational for transformation. Dr. Caroline Leaf explains that the brain is a physical organ made up of neurons, pathways, and chemicals, much like the hardware of a computer. It's tangible, can be scanned and operates within the realm of biology.

On the other hand, the mind is not physical. It is software that directs the brain. The mind is where you think, feel, choose, and process the world around you. It holds your will, emotions, and thoughts- essentially the driving force that shapes the physical structure of your brain. The brain is reactive, but the mind is proactive.

This is a profound revelation because it tells us one thing: **you are not a prisoner of your brain.** You have the God given power, through your mind, to renew and reshape it. Neuroscience calls this "neuroplasticity"- the ability of the brain to rewire itself based on the way you think, learn, and behave. What science is just now proving, scripture revealed centuries ago.

Romans 8:6 states, *"The mind governed by the flesh is death, but the mind governed by the Spirit is life and peace."* This verse underscores the vital truth that the spirit, not just the mind, plays a critical role in rewiring. The mind is the battleground where decisions are made, but the Holy Spirit equips us to align our thoughts with God's will.

## The Mind's Influence on Your Brain and Life

Every thought you think releases chemicals in your brain, either building healthy neural pathways or reinforcing destructive ones. If you constantly meditate on thoughts like, "I'm a failure,"your brain responds by strengthening pathways that perpetuate insecurity, stress, and fear. Your mind creates a reality that your brain reinforces.

Here's the good news: the opposite is also true. When you align your thoughts with God's Word, you trigger healing, growth, and peace. Positive, truthful thoughts begin to overwrite the toxic ones, creating new pathways that empower you to live fully. As you renew your mind, your brain's structure follows suit.

For example: consider Philippians 4:8

*"Finally, my brothers and sisters, whatever is true, whatever is noble, whatever is right, whatever is pure, whatever is lovely, whatever is admirable—if anything is excellent or praiseworthy—think about such things."*

This verse is not just a moral suggestion; it's a scientific blueprint for rewiring your mind. When you choose to focus on thoughts that are noble, true, and lovely, you direct your mind to produce peace instead of chaos.

## Spirit-Guided Transformation

While the mind influences the brain, the spirit influences the mind. You were never meant to fight this battle alone. Galatians 5:16 reminds us, "So I say, walk by the Spirit, and you will not gratify the desires of the flesh."The Holy Spirit empowers us to take control of our minds and align our thoughts with God's truth. Remember, this world is natural with natural and spiritual experiences.

When you invite The Lord and Savior Jesus Christ into your life, He doesn't just help you recognize toxic patterns, He gives you the strength to overcome them. As you pray, meditate on scripture, and renew your focus on God, your spirit begins to dominate your mind, and your mind transforms your brain. It's a beautiful, interconnected process: Spirit – Mind – Brain – Life.

He transforms not only what we think but how we think, helping us recognize and reject patterns that lead us away from God's purpose.

One keyway the Holy Spirit brings transformation is by illuminating areas of our thought life that are out of alignment with God's Word. This often comes through moments of conviction, where the Spirit reveals toxic patterns, lies we've believed, or fears we've allowed to take root. These moments are not meant to shame us but to lead us into freedom. As we surrender those areas to God, the Spirit gently reshapes our mindset, replacing fear with faith, doubt with confidence, and bitterness with forgiveness. This process requires humility and trust, but it leads to lasting renewal.

Furthermore, the Spirit equips us with supernatural strength to persist in the process of rewiring. Romans 8:26 reminds us that the Holy Spirit helps us in our weakness, even interceding for us when we don't know what to pray. In those moments when breaking toxic thought patterns feels overwhelming, the Spirit sustains us, offering encouragement and power beyond what we can achieve on our own. As we rely on Him, we are not only transformed ourselves but become agents of transformation for others, reflecting God's love and wisdom in every aspect of our lives.

By choosing to invite the Holy Spirit into your thought life daily, you are committing to a lifelong partnership that will bring healing, clarity, and strength. This divine collaboration ensures that your mind is continually renewed, your heart is aligned with God's truth, and your life becomes a reflection of His perfect will.

The mind is the gateway to transformation. In Proverbs 23:7 reminds us, *"For as a man thinks in his heart, so is he."* This verse highlights the profound influence of our thoughts on our identity and actions. Our mind is where decisions are made, perspectives are shaped, and beliefs take root. By allowing the Holy Spirit to guide our thought life, we align our thinking with God's truth, enabling us to walk in the freedom and purpose He has for us. This transformation can lead us closer to His plan for our lives. As the scriptures states in Jeremiah 29:11, *"For I know the plans I have for you,"* declares the Lord, *"plans to prosper you and not to harm you, plans to give you hope and a future."* This scripture highlights the fact that there are plans for us already in place and they are all good. Therefore, it's beneficial for us to align our thought pattern to a more positive foundation.

Science supports this spiritual truth. Research in cognitive-behavioral psychology reveals that our thought pattern has a profound impact on our emotions and actions. Negative thinking often leads to cycles of fear, anxiety, and hopelessness, while positive, truth-based thinking brings peace, focus, and resilience. Proverbs 4:23 says, *"Above all else, guard your heart, for everything you do flows from it."* In scripture, when it talks about the "heart", many times, it refers to the mind as well. The thoughts we allow to focus on eventually become a part of our lives and begin to bring to fruition the fruit of the thought pattern we have focused on. This is why Philippians 4:8 is imperative for us to take to heart, which tells us to focus on what is true, noble, right, pure, and lovely. By meditating on God's Word, we reinforce healthy thought patterns and uproot the lies of the enemy.

## The Brain's Neuroplasticity and Transformation

The brain is the physical organ that supports the mind's activity. Neuroscience has revealed the incredible concept of neuroplasticity, which is the brain's ability to reorganize and form new neural connections throughout life. This means that our thoughts can physically reshape our brains.

Every time you think, neurons in your brain fire and connect, forming pathways that become stronger with repetition. Toxic thought patterns, such as self-doubt, bitterness, or fear, can create deeply entrenched pathways, making them feel automatic. However, the good news is that these pathways can be replaced. When you choose to focus on God's Word, new, healthier pathways are formed, weakening the old ones.

Scripture reflects this concept beautifully. In 2 Corinthians 10:5, Paul says, "We demolish arguments and every pretension that sets itself up against the knowledge of God, and we take captive every thought to make it obedient to Christ." Taking thoughts captive involves interrupting toxic patterns and replacing them with God's promises. For example, a thought like "I'll never meet anyone," A powerful scripture to counter that thought Psalm 37:4 *"Take delight in the Lord, and He will give you the desires of your heart."* This verse reminds you that as you focus on relationship with God and trust in Him, He will provide for your needs, including meaningful relationships. It encourages you to release feelings of hopelessness and trust in His perfect timing and plan.

A study by Dr. Caroline Leaf, a cognitive neuroscientist, shows that intentional, faith-based meditation can significantly reduce stress and toxic thinking while improving focus and emotional health. This is a practical demonstration of the transformative power of aligning our minds with the Spirit.

## The Spirit as Our Guide

The Holy Spirit plays a critical role in connection between the mind and the brain. While science explains the mechanics of thought and behavior, it cannot replace the divine wisdom and healing that come through the Spirit. Jesus promised in John 14:26: *"But the Advocate, the Holy Spirit, whom the Father will send in my name, will teach you all things and will remind you of everything I have said to you."*

The Spirit not only brings comfort but also serves as a guide in identifying toxic thought patterns. Many times, we may not even realize the lies we've internalized until the Spirit illuminates them. For example, you may struggle with fear in certain areas of your life without realizing its root cause. The Holy Spirit gently brings clarity, pointing you to Scripture and providing the strength to confront those fears with God's truth.

Through prayer and daily communion with the Spirit, you invite supernatural insight into your mental and emotional health. This partnership bridges the gap between the spiritual and the physical, empowering you to walk in freedom and purpose.

# Practical Steps for Aligning Mind, Brain, and Spirit

### 1. Daily Meditation on scripture

Meditating on God's Word strengthens new neural pathways aligned with His truth. Psalm 1:2-3 describes the person who meditates on the Word as being like a tree planted by streams of water, yielding fruit in season and prospering in all they do.

Start each day by focusing on a specific verse. Repeat it throughout the day, reflecting on its meaning and application. This practice not only renews your mind but also reinforces positive, God-centered thought patterns.

### 2. Journaling Your Thoughts

Writing down your thoughts and aligning them with Scripture helps you identify and uproot toxic patterns. As Proverbs 4:23 says, "Above all else, guard you heart, for everything you do flows from it."Journaling provides a space to evaluate your mental state and replace harmful beliefs with truth.

### 3. Prayerful Reflection

Invite the Holy Spirit to reveal areas where your thoughts are not aligned with God's Word. Ask for wisdom, strength, and discernment to take captive every thought. This daily prayer not only renews your mind but also strengthen your relationship with God.

### 4. Gratitude Practice

Gratitude is scientifically proven to improve mental health and increase feelings of joy and contentment. In 1 Thessalonians 5:18, Paul writes, "Give thanks in all circumstances; for this is God's will for you in Christ Jesus." Begin or end each day by listing three things you are thankful for. This practice shifts your focus from what's lacking to what God already provided.

**5. Community Support**
Surround yourself with fellow believers who can encourage and
support you in your journey. Hebrews 10:24-25 reminds us to
spur one another on toward love and good deeds and not to give
up meeting together.

## Scriptural and Scientific Unity

The unity between scripture and science is evident in how the
mind, brain, and spirit work together. While science explains the
processes of neuroplasticity and the impact of thought on the brain,
scripture provides the wisdom and guidance necessary to direct those
thoughts toward truth.

For example, studies on gratitude show that it activates the brain's
reward centers, releasing chemicals like dopamine and serotonin that
promote happiness. This aligns with Philippians 4:6-7, which says:
*"Do not be anxious about anything, but in every situation, by prayer
and petition, with thanksgiving, present your requests to God, which
transcends all understanding, will guard your hearts and your minds in
Christ Jesus."* Science confirms that thankfulness rewires the brain to
promote peace, just as Scripture promises.

Similarly, forgiveness has been shown to reduce stress and improve
overall well-being. Ephesians 4:32 calls us to be kind and compassionate, forgiving one another just as Christ forgave us. The act of forgiveness not only aligns with God's Word but also liberates the mind and
brain from the toxic cycles of bitterness and anger.

## Walking in Wholeness

Aligning your mind, brain, and spirit is not a one-time event; it's a daily commitment to transformation. As you partner with the Holy Spirit, meditate on scripture, and apply practical steps to renew your mind, you'll experience greater clarity, peace, and purpose.

Your mind will begin to reflect God's truth, your brain will support healthier thought patterns, and your spirit will thrive in communion with the Holy Spirit. This comprehensive approach ensures that every area of your life, mental, emotional, and spiritual, aligns with God's perfect will, allowing you to walk in fullness of His promises.

## Reflection Questions

- What thoughts are currently governing your mind, thoughts of life and peace, or thoughts of fear and negativity?
- How often do you invite the Holy Spirit into your thought life?
- Write down three scriptures that focus on life, transformation, and renewal. Begin meditating on these daily.

**"The mind shapes the brain, the spirit renews the soul, and together they transform a life, proving that change begins within and flows into every part of our being."**

— Naomi

## Closing Prayer

Heavenly Father,

Thank You for the power You've given me to renew my mind. Help me to recognize that my thoughts hold the key to transformation and remind me that Your Holy Spirit equips me to overcome toxic patterns. Teach me to set my mind on the things above, on Your truth, peace, and love, so that my mind and brain align with your will.

Lord, I surrender my thoughts to You. Let Your Spirit lead me as I rewire my mind and walk in the freedom You promise. Transform my thinking so that I may experience life and peace in every area of my life.

In Jesus' name,

Amen.

# Chapter Four

## The Power of Words

*"Death and life are in the power of the tongue, and those who love it will eat its fruit."* -Proverbs 18:21

Words are more than just sounds we use to communicate; they are carriers of power. What you say whether to yourself or to others, has the ability to create, destroy, heal, or harm. In fact, your words don't just reflect your thoughts; they shape your thoughts and, ultimately, your reality.

This is why scripture places such emphasis on the words we speak. In Genesis, God used words to create the heavens and the earth, saying, *"Let there be light,"* and light came into existence. Made in His image, we too wield the ability to create through our words. Whether positive or negative, our speech influences how we see ourselves, how others perceive us, and how we experience the world.

This principle is not just spiritual but also deeply scientific. Neuroscience confirms that words, whether spoken or heard, directly impact our brains. Positive words stimulate the brain's prefrontal cortex, fostering creativity, resilience, and hope. Conversely, negative words trigger the brain's fear center, releasing stress hormones that hinder growth and healing.

In this chapter, we will explore how the words we choose, both internally and externally, can help rewire our minds for transformation. We will also uncover practical ways to align our speech with God's truth, using our words as tools to build, uplift, and empower ourselves and those around us.

## Words Shape Our Inner Dialogue

The most important conversations you'll ever have are the ones you have with yourself. Your internal dialogue sets the tone for how you interpret life's events and influences your mental, emotional, and even physical state. If your self-talk is filled with negativity like, *"I'm not good enough," "I'll always fail,"* or *"I'll never change,"* it reinforces toxic thought patterns that limit your growth.

On the other hand, when your self-talk aligns with God's Word, it rewires your brain to see possibilities, hope, and strength. Consider this: when you say, *"I can do all things through Christ who strengthens me"* (Philippians 4:13), you are not merely quoting verse. You are programming your mind to operate from a position of faith rather than fear. Repeating God's promises strengthens neural pathways associated with confidence, resilience, and peace, empowering you to move forward despite challenges.

## The Ripple Effect of Spoken Words

What we speak out loud has the potential to shape not only our lives but the lives of others. Words spoken in anger or frustration can leave wounds that last for years, while words of encouragement can inspire someone to believe in themselves and their God-given potential. Proverbs 16:24 says, *"Gracious words are a honeycomb, sweet to the soul and healing to the bones."*

Think of a time when someone spoke life-giving words over you. Perhaps they called out a gift or talent in you that you hadn't noticed, or they encouraged you during a tough season. Those words carried a weight that influenced your actions and confidence. Now consider the opposite, a moment when someone's harsh or careless words left you feeling defeated or inadequate. Such is the power of the tongue.

## Words Produce Tangible Impact

Science confirms that words have a tangible impact on our mental and emotional well-being. Studies in psychology and neuroscience show that positive words stimulate the brain's reward centers, release dopamine and serotonin, chemicals that enhance mood, motivation, and overall health. Conversely, negative words activate the brain's amygdala, triggering a stress response that releases cortisol, which can lead to anxiety and even impair cognitive function. This scientific evidence underscores the profound truth of Proverbs 16:24: "Gracious words are a honeycomb, sweet to the soul and healing to the bones." Spoken words are not just sounds; they have the power to influence both the mind and the body.

# The Weight of Words: Building Up or Tearing Down

As previously mentioned, words are not merely sounds; they carry weight, influence, and the power to shape lives. As Proverbs 18:21 reminds us: *"The tongue has the power of life and death, and those who love it will eat its fruit."* This scripture underscores a profound truth: the words we speak can breathe life into someone's spirit or crush it entirely.

Reflect on the times when a kind word lifted your spirits or gave you the courage to take a step forward. Maybe a teacher told you that you had potential, inspiring you to pursue a career or talent you had doubted. Or perhaps a friend's encouragement in a dark season reminded you of your worth. These moments are not coincidences; they are the ripple effects of life-giving words.

On the other hand, harsh words can leave scars that linger far beyond the moment they are spoken. A single careless comment, like "You'll never amount to anything," can echo in someone's mind for years, influencing their confidence and decisions. Just as a ripple in water spreads outward, the effect of our words extends far beyond the initial moment.

Scientific Proof: How Words Impact the Brain

Science backs up what scripture teaches about the power of words. Research in neuroscience reveals that positive and negative words directly affect our brain chemistry. Positive words stimulate the release of dopamine and serotonin, chemicals associated with happiness, motivation, and overall well-being. They can literally light up the reward centers in our brain, reinforcing feelings of encouragement and hope which are called neurotransmitters.

Conversely, negative words trigger stress responses in the brain, releasing cortisol, the stress hormone which is amygdala activation. Chronic exposure to negative language, whether from others or in our own self-talk, can lead to heightened anxiety, reduced cognitive function, and even depression.

In a famous study, Japanese researcher Dr. Masaru Emoto demonstrated the power of words on water molecules. When exposed to positive words like "love" and "gratitude," the water formed beautiful, symmetrical crystals. In contrast, exposure to negative words like "hate" caused chaotic and disfigured patterns. While humans are far more complex than water, the principle still applies: the energy of our words can either bring harmony or disruption. Proverbs 25:11 says, "A word fitly spoken is like apples of gold in settings of silver."This verse highlights the beauty and value of speaking words that are appropriate, timely, and uplifting. It reminds us that well-chosen words have the power to bring grace and encouragement to others. It's good for the soul (the mind, will, and emotion).

## Words as Seeds: What Are You Planting?

Imagine every word you speak as a seed planted in someone's heart. Over time, those seeds grow, producing fruit that reflects the nature of the words.

- **Positive Seeds:**Words like "I believe in you," "You are loved," or "You have a gift" can cultivate confidence, perseverance, and hope in the lives of others.
- **Negative Seeds:**Conversely, words like "You're not good enough" or "You'll never succeed" can plant doubt, fear, and insecurity.

In Luke 6:45, Jesus teaches, *"A good man brings good things out of the good stored up in his heart, and an evil man brings evil things out of the evil stored up in his heart. For the mouth speaks what the heart is full of.* " This reminds us that our words reveal the condition of our hearts. If we store up kindness, gratitude, and love, our words will reflect those qualities.

Consider daily conversations. What seeds are you planting in your children, your spouse, your friends, and even strangers? Are your words cultivating life or unintentionally sowing harm?

## The Echo of Encouragement

Encouragement doesn't just lift someone in the moment; it creates ripples that can carry them through seasons of doubt or hardship. Consider the story of Barnabas in the Bible. Known as the "Son of Encouragement," Barnabas used his words and actions to uplift others.

In Acts 9, when Paul (then Saul) faced skepticism from the apostles after his conversion, it was Barnabas who vouched for him and spoke on his behalf. The act of encouragement helped Paul step into his calling, ultimately leading to the spread of the gospel across the world. Barnabas's words didn't just affect Paul; they had a ripple effect on countless lives touched by Paul's ministry.

Likewise, our words of encouragement may seem small, but their impact can be far-reaching. You never know how a kind word might influence someone's decision to keep going, pursue a dream, or simply believe in themselves again.

## Healing From Hurtful Words

While life-giving words can uplift, the wounds left by harsh words are often deeper and harder to heal. Proverbs 12:18 says, "The words of the reckless pierce like swords, but the tongue of the wise brings healing." If you've been hurt by reckless words, it's important to recognize that healing is possible.

**1. Identify the Lie:** Often, hurtful words plant lies about our worth or identity. Ask God to reveal any lies you've internalized and replace them with His truth.

- **Example:** If someone told you, "You're a failure," replace that with Jeremiah 29:11. "For I know the plans I have for you," declares the Lord, "plans to prosper you and not to harm you, plans to give you hope and a future."

**2. Forgive the Speaker:**Forgiveness doesn't excuse the hurtful words, but it frees you from carrying the weight of them. Ephesians 4:32 encourages us to "be kind and compassionate to one another, forgiving each other, just as in Christ God forgave you."

As believers, we are called to steward our words wisely. Ephesians 4:29 challenges us: "Do not let any unwholesome talk come out of our mouths, but only what is helpful for building others up according to their needs." Speaking intentionally, whether to yourself, your family, or your community, is one of the most effective ways to reflect God's love and truth.

# Practical Steps to Transform Your Words

1. **Speak Scripture Over Your Life:**Replace negative self-talk with the promises of God. Write down key verses that address areas where you struggle, whether it's fear, doubt, or insecurity, and speak to them aloud daily. For example, if you feel overwhelmed, declare Isaiah 41:10: "Do not fear, for I am with you; do not be dismayed, for I am your God. I will strengthen you and help you; I will uphold you with my righteous right hand." Speaking God's Word not only aligns your thoughts with His truth but also reshapes your neural pathways, reinforcing faith over fear.

2. **Practice Gratitude in Your Speech:**Words of gratitude can shift your mindset from scarcity to abundance. Start each day by speaking out loud at least three things you are thankful for. Gratitude reorients your thoughts toward the good in your life and strengthens neural connections that foster positivity and resilience.

3. **Guard Against Negative Speech:**Be intentional about eliminating toxic words from your vocabulary, whether they are directed at yourself or others. This includes complaints, gossip, or self-deprecating humor. Instead, ask yourself, "Does what I'm about to say bring life or harm?"Training yourself to speak with kindness and purpose creates an environment of growth and peace, both within and around you.

4. **Encourage Others Regularly:**Make it a habit to speak life over the people in your sphere of influence. Call out their strengths, affirm their efforts, and remind them of their worth in Christ. By doing so, you not only uplift them but also reinforce a positive and generous mindset within yourself.

## The Creative Power of God's Word

God created the universe with His words: *"And God said, 'Let there be light,' and there was light"* (Genesis 1:3). As His image-bearers, we share in this creative power, albeit on a smaller scale. Our words have the ability to shape our reality and influence the outcomes we experience.

This doesn't mean our words are magical or that we can manipulate reality to fit our desires. Instead, it reflects the principle that what we consistently speak reflects the beliefs we hold, and those beliefs shape our actions. If you repeatedly declare, *"I am capable and equipped because God is with me,"* you're far more likely to step into challenging situations with confidence than if you constantly say, *"I can't do this."*

James 3:4 compares the tongue to a small rudder that steers a large ship. It may be tiny, but it determines the direction of your life. If you want to transform your mind and your future, begin by transforming your words. Speak life, speak truth, and speak in alignment with God's promises.

This principle resonates both spiritually and scientifically. Neuroscience confirms that spoken words impact neural pathways, reinforcing thoughts and beliefs that guide our decisions and actions. If we consistently speak negativity, doubt, and fear, we program our minds to follow those paths. Conversely, speaking God's truth, declaring His promises and aligning our words with His Word, redirects our lives toward His purposes, producing hope, peace, and transformation.

To transform your mind and your future, begin by transforming your words. Speak life, speak truth, and speak in alignment with God's promises. Declare His Word over your circumstances, regardless of what you see in the natural. When you speak God's Word, you are releasing His power into your life and situations, much like how He spoke creation into existence. By doing so, you align your heart, mind, and spirit with His divine will, inviting His supernatural power to work through you.

## The Eternal Ripple Effect

The ripple effect of spoken words extends beyond this life. In Matthew 12:35, Jesus says, *"But I tell you that everyone will give account on the day of judgement for every empty word they have spoken."* This verse serves as both a warning and a reminder of eternal significance of our words.

Words have the power to shape destinies, transform relationships, and advance God's kingdom. Whether it's encouraging a friend teaching a child, or sharing the gospel with a stranger, your words can leave a lasting legacy.

As you go about your day, remember that your words are not just sounds, they are seeds, ripples, and reflections of your heart. Choose to use them wisely, and watch as they create waves of life, love, and transformation. Every word you speak carries the power to build or break, to heal or hurt, and to uplift or tear down. When you choose words of faith, encouragement, and truth, you plant seeds that bear fruit. All words are fruit bearing, whether intentional or by happenstance.

In the next chapter, we will explore how to dismantle the lies that often take root in our minds and replace them with the liberating truth of God's Word. But for now, let us reflect: What words are shaping your life today? Are they words of life, or are they words of limitation: The choice is yours.

**"Words are seeds of life; they create ripples in the soul, effecting
and shaping the mind, building up or tearing down, and planting
the future we live in."**

— Naomi

## Closing Prayer:

Heavenly Father,

May I not become complacent in the stillness but speak encouraging words that uplift and encourage someone today. May I be
mindful of the words I use knowing that the effect of what I speak has
an impact that far exceeds the moment in which it was spoken. Teach
me Lord to speak words that are seasoned with grace so that I am
pleasing to you. As I glorify your name, may I be mindful to stay the
course that honors you the most. I thank you Lord for helping me
understand the importance of my spoken words and the effect they
have on all who are under the sound of my voice when I speak.

In Jesus' name, Amen.

# Chapter Five

## Rewiring Your Brain with God's Design



Your brain is one of the most extraordinary creations of God, designed with the ability to adapt, grow, and change. This concept, known as neuroplasticity, refers to the brain's ability to form new neural connections throughout our life. Science has proven that thoughts you focus on most frequently shape these neural pathways, strengthening certain patterns while weakening others. In other words, your mind literally has the power to rewire your brain, creating new habits and breaking old ones.

This scientific truth aligns beautifully with scripture. Romans 12:2 tells us to be "transformed by the renewing of your mind." The renewing process involves more than just positive thinking, it's a deliberate effort to align your thoughts with God's truth, rejecting lies and embracing His promises. Neuroscience confirms that the thoughts you choose to meditate on can physically change the structure of your brain, influencing not only how you think but also how you feel and act.

Dr. Caroline Leaf, a neuroscientist and Christian author, explains that toxic thoughts, such as fear, anger, and doubt, create unhealthy patterns in the brain that can lead to anxiety, depression, and even physical illness. However, focusing on positive, God-centered thoughts can reverse this damage, promoting healing and renewal. This is because the brain is not static; it's dynamic and constantly responding to what you choose to feed it.

## The Science of Rewiring

When you think a thought repeatedly, neurons in your brain form stronger connections. For example, if you habitually think, *"I'm not good enough,"* the neural pathway for that thought becomes stronger, making it easier for your brain to default to that pattern. Conversely, when you intentionally replace that thought with God's truth, *"I am fearfully and wonderfully made"*(Psalm 139:14), you begin to weaken the negative pathway while building a new, positive one.

This process requires consistency. Neuroscience suggests it takes at least 21 days to begin breaking down old neural pathways and replacing them with new ones. The more you reinforce God's truth in your mind, the more automatic it becomes. This is why meditating on scripture is so powerful, it transforms your thinking while literally rewiring your brain to align with God's design.

# The Role of Focus in Brain Rewiring

One of the key factors in rewiring your brain is focus. What you give attention to grows stronger in your mind. This is why the Bible emphasizes fixing our thoughts on what is true, noble, right, pure, and admirable (Philippians 4:8). When you intentionally focus on God's promises, your brain begins to prioritize those thoughts, forming stronger and healthier neural pathways. Conversely, when you dwell on fear, shame, or negative experiences, those unhealthy pathways are reinforced, making it harder to break free from destructive patterns

Neuroscientists have found that the brain's ability to change is most effective when paired with deep, intentional focus. This means that simply reading or hearing the truth isn't enough; you must actively engage with it. For example, meditating on scripture, journaling your thoughts, or declaring affirmations out loud helps solidify God's truth in your brain. Over time, this practice doesn't just transform your mindset, it influences your emotions and actions, enabling you to live in greater alignment with God's plan for your life.

# Aligning Your Thoughts with Divine Purpose

The brain, a complex organ that governs our thoughts, emotions, and actions, functions as the command center of the body. It communicates with the rest of the body through billions of neurons, forming neural pathways that transmit signals between the brain and the body. Key areas of the brain, such as prefrontal cortex, amygdala, and hippocampus, play specific roles in decision-making, emotional regulation, and memory. Proverbs 4:23 says, *"Keep thy heart with all diligence; for out of it are the issues of life."* In biblical times, the "heart" often referred to the inner man, which includes the mind and thoughts. This scripture aligns with neuroscience, showing that what we focus on shapes the brain's structure and influences every action we take on a daily basis.

The amygdala, often called the brain's "fear center," is responsible for processing emotions like fear and stress. When we dwell on negative or fearful thoughts, the amygdala triggers the body's fight-or-flight response, releasing stress hormones like cortisol. Prolonged activation of this response can lead to physical issues such as high blood pressure, weakened immunity, and even brain damage over time. However, scripture teaches us to combat fear and anxiety with God's peace. Philippians 4:6-7 states, "Be careful for nothing; but in every thing by prayer and supplication with thanksgiving let your requests be made known unto God. And the peace of God, which passeth all understanding, shall keep your hearts and minds through Christ Jesus." This peace calms the amygdala and helps regulate the body physically, reducing harmful stress.

The prefrontal cortex, located at the front of the brain, is where higher-ordering thinking, decision-making, and self-control occur. This region receives input from both emotional and rational areas of the brain, creating a balance between impulsivity and wisdom. Science reveals that repeated focus on positive, purposeful thoughts strengthens the prefrontal cortex, leading to better self-regulation and decision-making. Romans 8:5 reinforces this: "For they that are after the flesh do mind the things of the flesh; but they that are after the Spirit the things of the Spirit." By aligning our thoughts with the Spirit, we not only improve spiritual focus but also enhance the brain's ability to guide us toward godly decisions.

The hippocampus, critical for memory and learning, is highly responsive to what we meditate on. Chronic negativity or stress can shrink the hippocampus, impairing memory and increasing susceptibility to depression. Conversely, meditating on God's Word strengthens this region, fostering resilience and mental clarity. Psalm 1:2-3 describes the benefits of such meditation: "But his delight is in the law of the Lord; and in his law doth he meditate day and night. And he shall be like a tree planted by the rivers of water." This scripture mirrors the scientific finding that meditation can grow healthy neural pathways, much like a well-nourished tree flourishes.

Physically, the brain's signals influence every part of the body through the nervous system. For instance, gratitude and worship activate the brain's dopaminergic pathways, releasing dopamine, a "feel-good" neurotransmitter that reduces pain and improves mood. 1 Corinthians 6:19-20 reminds us that our bodies, including our brains, are temples of the Holy Spirit: "What? Know ye not that your body is the temple of the Holy Ghost which is in you?" By aligning our thoughts and behaviors with God's design, we honor Him both spiritually and physically. This divine alignment promotes not only spiritual transformation but also physical healing, revealing the intricate connection between the mind, brain, and body.

## Building Habits of Renewal

Another important aspect of brain rewiring is creating habits that reinforce healthy thought patterns. Your brain thrives on repetition, which is why daily practices like prayer, gratitude, and scripture meditation are so transformative. Each time you engage in these habits, you are training your brain to rely on God's truth rather than defaulting to old, toxic patterns.

Even small changes can have a significant impact. For instance, starting your day by declaring a verse like *"God has not given me the spirit of fear, but of power, love, and a sound mind"* (2 Timothy 1:7) sets the tone for how your brain processes challenges throughout the day. These habits don't just shape your brain, they also shift your perspective, allowing you to see your circumstances through the lens of God's promises.

As you embrace these practices, remember that the process of renewing your mind is both spiritual and scientific. You are partnering with God in a way that honors the incredible design He gave your brain while also leaning on His supernatural power to bring about lasting transformation.

**"Align your thoughts with God's purpose to rewire your mind."**

## Reflections

1. **What thoughts or beliefs have I been focusing on that may not align with God's truth?** Reflect on whether your dominant thought patterns are rooted in faith and hope or in fear and negativity.
2. **How can I intentionally incorporate scripture and God's promises into my daily thoughts and habits?** Consider practical steps, such as meditating on a verse, journaling affirmations, or praying specifically about areas where your thoughts need renewal.
3. **What habits or thought patterns am I reinforcing in my life, and are they helping or hindering my transformation?** Identify whether your current routines and self-talk are strengthening positive neural pathways or reinforcing toxic ones.

**"To rewire your brain with God's design is to align your thoughts with His purpose, letting His truth reshape your mind, focus your path, and renew your spirit."**

— Naomi

## Closing Prayer

Heavenly Father,

Thank you for creating our minds with such incredible potential for renewal and transformation. We are in awe of how intricately You designed our brains, giving us the ability to align our thoughts with Your truth. Lord, help us to identify and replace the lies that have taken root in our minds with promises found in Your Word. Teach us to focus on what is good, pure, and holy, and guide us as we build habits that honor You.

We ask for the strength to persevere in this journey of rewiring our thoughts and the patience to trust the process, knowing that You are at work within us. Fill our hearts with hope, our minds with peace, and our spirits with courage as we step into the abundant life You've prepared for us.

In Jesus' name

Amen.

# Chapter Six

## From Chains To Change: How Science and Faith Unite to Break Strongholds

*We demolish arguments and every pretension that sets itself up against the knowledge of God, and we take captive every thought to make it obedient to Christ." (2 Corinthians 10:5) NIV*

In this chapter, we explore the vital process of identifying toxic thought patterns and learning how to replace them with truth-filled, life-giving beliefs. Both Scripture and science affirm that our thoughts shape our lives. These mental cycles can create neural pathways that determine how we think, feel, and act. Thankfully, the brain's capacity for change, known as neuroplasticity, means that these patterns are not permanent. With intentionality and faith, we can transform our minds and lives.

## The Science of Thought Patterns

To understand the significance of toxic thoughts, it helps to examine the science behind them. Every thought you think produces an electrical impulse in your brain, creating neural pathways. Repeated thoughts strengthen these pathways, much like a trail becomes defined the more it is walked on. Negative patterns, such as fear, self-doubt, or anger, become "default settings in your mind when revisited often.

Dr. Caroline Leaf, a cognitive neuroscientist, explains this process by comparing toxic thoughts to trees in the brain. Healthy thoughts look like flourishing green trees, while toxic thoughts resemble blackened, shriveled trees. Over time, these toxic trees can impact mental and physical health, leading to anxiety, depression, or even physical illness.

The good news is that the brain can heal and change. Through intentional focus, we can create new, healthy neural pathways and prune away the toxic ones. This process aligns with Romans 12:2: *"Do not conform to the pattern of this world but be transformed by the renewing of your mind."* Science is catching up to what scripture has long taught: transformation begins in the mind. That's why the bible has so many scriptures concerning thoughts, words, mind renewal and even how we should think which inherently will rewire our minds and realign us to how we were originally meant to think.

## Replacing Lies with Truth

Toxic thought patterns often originate from lies we've believed about ourselves, others, or even God. These lies might stem from past experiences, cultural influences, or inner fears. They grow stronger every time we agree with them, reinforcing the negative neural pathways in our brain.

The process of replacing lies with truth begins with identifying the lies. Ask yourself:

- What recurring negative thoughts do I have?

- Where did these beliefs originate?
- Are these thoughts rooted in truth or fear?

Once identified, replace each lie with truth, grounded in scripture. For instance:

- **Lie:**"I'm not good enough."
- **Truth:**"I am fearfully and wonderfully made" (Psalm 139:14).

When you meditate on these truths, you activate new neural pathways. Neuroscience reveals that repeated focus on positive thoughts strengthens these pathways, making the truth your new default setting.

## How Science and Scripture Work Together

Neuroscience shows that it takes about 21 days to form a new neural pathway and approximately 63 days for it to become a habit. This scientific insight underscores the importance of consistency. Scripture mirrors this in passages like Joshua 1:8, which emphasizes meditating on God's Word both day and night for lasting transformation.

Moreover, brain scans reveal that gratitude and prayer can shift brain activity from the amygdala (the fear center) to the prefrontal cortex (responsible for rational decision making). This aligns with Philippians 4:6-7: *"Do not be anxious about anything, but in every situation, by prayer and petition, with thanksgiving, present your requests to God."*

God designed our brains with the capacity for renewal, allowing us to experience both spiritual and physical freedom when we align our thoughts with His truth.

## Practical Steps to Break the Cycle

1. **Recognize Toxic Thoughts:**Keep a journal to track recurring negative thoughts. Awareness is the first step to change.
2. **Challenge the Lies:**Questions whether your thoughts align with truth or fear. Use scripture as your ultimate standard.
3. **Replace with Truth:**For each negative thought, find a corresponding Bible verse or affirmation and repeat it daily.
4. **Visualize Growth:**Picture your mind as a garden. Each time you choose a positive thought, imagine planting a seed that will grow into a flourishing tree.
5. **Practice Gratitude and Prayer:**These habits calm the brain and foster positive neural activity.

## Looking Ahead

In the next chapter, we will delve deeper into dismantling lies and uncovering the truths that set us free. Through scripture and scientific principles, we will explore actionable tools to create lasting change in our thought patterns. But before moving forward, take a moment to reflect on your current thought life.

**"Breaking strongholds begins with renewing your mind through truth and faith."**

— Naomi

## Closing Prayer

Heavenly Father,

Thank You for designing our minds with the ability to change and grow. Reveal the toxic thought patterns that have taken root in our lives. Help us to identify and replace them with Your truth. Strengthen our hearts to persevere as we cultivate new, life-giving thoughts. May Your Word renew our minds and guide us into the abundant life You have planned for us.

In Jesus' name, Amen.

# Chapter Seven

## Dismantling Lies, Discovering Truth



Our minds are powerful, capable of building entire worlds through the stories we tell ourselves. Yet, many of these stories are shaped by lies and false beliefs about who we are, our worth, or our potential. These lies create mental strongholds, trapping us in patterns of fear, doubt, and negativity. But here's the good news: we are not powerless. Scripture tells us, *"Then you will know the truth, and the truth will set you free"* (John 8:32). And science supports this, revealing that our brains are not fixed; they are malleable, capable of rewiring through intentional focus and practice. In this chapter, we'll combine timeless spiritual truths with cutting-edge scientific principles to uncover how we can dismantle lies and replace them with truths that bring freedom and transformation.

To begin, we must first identify the lies that have taken root in our thinking. These may come from childhood experiences, societal pressures, or even well-meaning but misguided influences. For example, lies like "I'm not good enough" or "change is impossible" create neural pathways in our brains that become stronger the more we believe and act on them. However, neuroscience shows us the power of neuroplasticity, which is the brain's ability to reorganize itself by forming new connections. This aligns with the biblical command to "be transformed by renewing of your mind" (Romans 12:2). Through intentional reflection, scripture meditation, and practical tools, we can weaken old, destructive pathways and build new ones grounded in truth. In the pages that follow, we"ll explore actionable tools for replacing lies with truth and creating thought patterns that align with who God created us to be.

The process of dismantling lies, and uncovering truth isn't something we can do alone; it requires the power and guidance of the Holy Spirit. Jesus promised in John 16:13, *"But when He, the Spirit of truth, comes, He will guide you into all truth."* The Holy Spirit acts as both a counselor and a convictor, but never condemns, shining light on areas in our minds where lies have taken hold and empowering us to embrace God's truth. This divine partnership is essential because the lies we've believed often feel deeply ingrained, and it takes supernatural strength to confront and replace them. As we invite the Holy Spirit into this process, He not only reveals truth but also equips us with the wisdom and courage to walk in it daily.

Practically, this means approaching the process with prayerful intentionality. For example, when a negative or self-defeating thought arises, we can pause and ask the Holy Spirit to reveal its source and its truth. This is where scripture and science converge beautifully. Through tools like thought journaling, we can record the lies we've been thinking and replace them with scriptural affirmations, truths inspired by the Spirit. Over time, as we repeatedly engage in this practice the scripture encourages us to do, our brains begin to rewire, forming new pathways aligned with truth. Neuroscience confirms that repeated, intentional focus on positive truths strengthens new neural connections, making them our default way of thinking. The Holy Spirit empowers this process by continually guiding and reminding us of God's promises, helping us to align our minds with His truth and experience lasting freedom.

As we begin to renew our minds through the power of the Holy Spirit, it's important to remember that transformation is a journey, not an overnight fix. The process of breaking down deeply rooted lies and building new, truthful thought patterns requires consistent effort and patience. The enemy often tries to discourage us by reminding us of our past failures or telling us that change is too difficult. But this is where the Holy Spirit becomes our source of strength. Philippians 4:13 assures us, *"I can do all things through Christ who strengthens me."* With the Holy Spirit as our guide, we are equipped to overcome the barriers of old thinking and embrace the freedom that comes with aligning our thoughts with God's truth. The more we surrender to His guidance, the more we will see lasting change in how we think, feel, and live.

In addition to scripture and prayer, science offers practical tools that help us engage with the process of transformation. One such tool is cognitive behavioral techniques (CBT), which involve identifying and challenging negative thoughts and replacing them with healthier, more accurate ones. This aligns with the biblical principle of *taking every thought captive to make it obedient to Christ* (2 Corinthians 10:5). The Holy Spirit works through these methods, bringing them to life in a way that leads to genuine, lasting change. By intentionally choosing to focus on truth and reject the lies that have held us captive, we partner with God to rewire our brains and build thought patterns that lead to peace, joy, and fulfillment. As we allow the Holy Spirit to lead us through this process, we become more fully aligned with the person God created us to be, reflecting His truth in every area of our lives.

## Identifying and Confronting the Lies

In order to experience true transformation, we must first recognize the lies that have shaped our thinking. These false beliefs are often subtle and can stem from various sources: childhood experiences, societal expectations, or even personal failures. Some of the most common lies include, "I'm not worthy of love," "I will never be good enough," or "God is angry with me." These thoughts may have become so ingrained that they feel like truth, but they are not. The first step in dismantling these lies is to expose them for what they are, deceptions designed to keep us from living in the freedom God has for us. By inviting the Holy Spirit to reveal false beliefs, we allow God to shine light into the dark corner of our minds, setting us on the path to healing and wholeness.

## Replacing Lies with Truth

Once we've identified the lies, the next step is to replace them with God's truth. Romans 12:2 encourages us to "be transformed by the renewing of your mind." This is an intentional process that requires us to actively choose truth over the lies we've believed. Scripture is the ultimate source of truth, and as we meditate on God's Word, we begin to replace false beliefs with His promises. For example, if the lie is, "I am not worthy of love," the truth from scripture is, "For God so loved the world..." (John 3:16). The more we focus on these truths, the more our minds are renewed, and our perspective shifts. The process also involves being patient with ourselves and trusting the Holy Spirit to guide us through each step.

## The Role of Neuroplasticity in Transformation

Scientific principles support what scripture already reveals: our brains have the incredible ability to change. This phenomenon, known as neuroplasticity, refers to the brain's ability to form new neural connections throughout our lives. Just as we can form new habits through repeated actions, we can rewire our thought patterns through consistent focus on truth. When we choose to reject old, negative thought patterns and replace them with God's Word, we are essentially rewiring our brains. This is not an instantaneous process; it takes time and repetition. But the more we immerse ourselves in truth, the stronger these new neural pathways become. Through neuroplasticity, the transformation of our minds is not just spiritual; it's also neurological, making it possible to break free from old patterns and create new, healthy ways of thinking.

## Walking In Freedom

The final step in this process is to walk in the freedom that comes from living according to truth. This means allowing the Holy Spirit to continue guiding us, even after we've identified and replaced the lies. Transformation is an ongoing process, but as we consistently align our thoughts with God's Word and trust in the Holy Spirit's power, we began to experience lasting change. Walking in freedom doesn't mean that we will never encounter challenges or negative thoughts again, but it does mean that we have the tools and the power to recognize them for what they are and replace them with God's truth. As we continue to renew our minds, we move closer to the person God created us to be, and we experience the peace and joy that comes from living in His truth.

## Reflections

**1. What lies have I believed about myself, others, or God that may be holding me back?**
Take time to reflect on recurring negative thoughts or beliefs that might have become part of your identity. Ask the Holy Spirit to reveal areas where you've been deceived and begin identifying truths from scripture to counter those lies.

**2. How can I partner with both scripture and science to renew my mind?**
Consider the tools and strategies discussed in this chapter, such as meditating on God's Word, thought journaling, and leveraging the principles of neuroplasticity. Reflect on how intentional actions combined with spiritual guidance can create lasting change in your thought patterns.

**3. Am I allowing the Holy Spirit to guide me into freedom daily?**
Reflect on your relationship with the Holy Spirit and how much you lean on Him for strength, guidance, and wisdom in transforming your mind. Are there areas in your life where you need to surrender more fully to His leading?

**4. How can I use the principles of neuroplasticity to actively reshape my thought patterns?**
Reflect on the scientific understanding that your brain is capable of change through repeated focus and intentional effort. Consider practical ways to apply this knowledge, such as journaling positive truths, practicing gratitude, or imagining new, healthy thought patterns. How can you combine these techniques with scripture and prayer to reinforce lasting transformation in your mind?

"**Freedom begins when you replace lies with truth and renew your mind.**"

— Naomi

## Closing Prayer

Heavenly Father,

Thank you for the gift of a mind that can be renewed and reshaped. Help me to use the wisdom from both scripture and science to create thought patterns that honor You and bring peace to my life. Strengthen me in moments of doubt and remind me that You are always with me, leading me into freedom. May Your truth set me free and transform my life so that I can reflect Your love and grace to the world.

In Jesus' name, Amen.

# Chapter Eight

## Break Free: Building Resilience and Renewing Your Spirit

---

*"But those who hope in the Lord will renew their strength. They will soar on wings like eagles; they will run and not grow weary; they will walk and not be faint" (Isaiah 40:31)*

---

Freedom is not just about breaking away from the lies that hold us back; it's about building the resilience to stay free and the spiritual strength to thrive in every season of life. Scripture reminds us, *"Let us throw off everything that hinders and the sin that so easily entangles. And let us run with perseverance the race marked out for us"*(Hebrews 12:1). Resilience is the ability to persevere despite challenges, and God's Word gives us the foundation to develop it. In this chapter, we'll explore how to cultivate resilience, both mentally and spiritually, so we can navigate life's difficulties without reverting to old patterns. By combining the truth of scripture with insights from neuroscience, we'll uncover practical strategies for strengthening our inner resolve and renewing our spirit daily. With the Holy Spirit's guidance, we can fully embrace the abundant life God has promised us.

Resilience is the mind's remarkable ability to recover and adapt in the face of challenges, and science shows that it is not an innate trait but a skill that can be cultivated. Neuroplasticity, the brain's capacity to rewire itself, plays a crucial role in building resilience. When God fearfully and wonderfully created us, he included this ability, this resilience capability, this rewiring mechanism. With the help of the Holy Spirit through His Word, the possibility of successfully rewiring is very high if we apply God's Word and work the process. Studies reveal that consistent mindfulness practices, such as meditation or even deep breathing, strengthen the prefrontal cortex, the area responsible for decision making, emotional regulation, and problem-solving. This rewiring not only enhances mental flexibility but also dampens overactivity in the amygdala, the brain's fear, pleasure and anger center. By training the brain to respond rather than act, individuals develop greater emotional control, allowing them to handle stress with clarity and grace. Research published in Psychological Science confirms that people who practice cognitive reframing, viewing setbacks as opportunities to grow, experience decreased levels of cortisol, the stress hormone, which supports long-term mental and physical well-being. As Proverbs 4:23 reminds us, *"Above all else, guard your heart, for everything you do flows from it,"* emphasizing the importance of protecting and renewing our minds in the face of life's struggles. *"On another note, under a different subject, dealing with the mind can also be a spiritual struggle that can only be dealt with through prayer and deliverance."* But for the most part, most of us are just not doing the work through the process that can change and rewire our mindset, our thought process, our thoughts which can ultimately change our lives.

Building resilience also requires intentional efforts to renew the spirit. Positive psychology highlights the power of gratitude, optimism, and connection in strengthening the mind's ability to bounce back. Expressing gratitude shifts the brain's focus from negativity to abundance, creating a more balanced and hopeful outlook. Moreover, regular social interaction activates the release of oxytocin, the "bonding hormone," which mitigates feelings of isolation and strengthens emotional endurance. A study from the University of Pennsylvania found that individuals who actively practiced optimism and gratitude experienced significant increase in their overall resilience scores. When combined with a faith-based perspective, such as relying on scripture or prayer, this renewal process is amplified. Isaiah 40:31 promises, *"But those who hope in the Lord will renew their strength. They will soar on wings like eagles; they will run and not grow weary; they will walk and not faint."* By anchoring the mind to positive, life-giving practices and God's Word, individuals not only break free from the weight of adversity but also develop the strength to face future challenges with renewed vigor.

## Overcoming the Chains of Fear and Doubt

Overcoming the chains of fear and doubt is essential for living a life aligned with God's purpose. Scripture assures us that fear does not come from God. 2 Timothy 1:7 says, "For God has not given us a spirit of fear, but of power and love and of a sound mind." This verse emphasizes that fear is not a part of God's plan for His children. Instead, He has equipped us with power, love, and a sound mind, which enables us to overcome the grip of fear. Embracing truth, we can resist the natural inclination toward anxiety and live in the freedom that comes from God's promises.

Science also supports the idea that fear is not something we were meant to live with continuously. Research in neuroscience has shown that the brain can be rewired through intentional thought patterns, the process known as neuroplasticity. When we allow negative, fear-based thoughts to dominate our minds, we reinforce neural pathways that increase anxiety. However, by consistently replacing those thoughts with affirmations of God's Word, we can rewire our brains, creating new, healthier patterns that lead to peace and courage. The more we speak God's truth over fears, the more we reshape our minds to reflect

His love and power. The fear will begin to lessen over time, inserting more courage, power, peace, and love.

Jesus often spoke directly to the fear and doubt in people's hearts, encouraging them to trust in God's faithfulness. In Matthew 14:31, when Peter began to sink while walking on water, Jesus immediately reached out to him, saying, "You of little faith, why did you doubt?" This moment reveals how doubt can cause us to lose focus on God's power and promises. Jesus was reminding Peter that as long as we keep our eyes on Him, we have the strength to overcome any fear. Doubt is the enemy of faith, and when we doubt God's promises, we allow fear to rule our hearts and minds. Consistency is crucial, even when we can't trace what is happening or any changes occurring, consistent in speaking God's promises will eventually allow the manifestation of what we are speaking to come to fruition.

Science also acknowledges the power of faith over fear, especially in moments of stress. Studies have shown that when people practice mindfulness, trust, or prayer, their stress responses decrease, and they experience lower levels of cortisol, the hormone associated with stress. This is significant because cortisol impairs immune function and increases the risk of diseases when levels remain high for prolonged periods of time. Trusting In God's ability to handle our fears not only strengthens our spiritual life but also has tangible benefits for our physical well-being. Our bodies respond positively when we choose faith over fear, reinforcing the idea that overcoming fear is both a spiritual and physiological process.

Moreover, overcoming fear involves understanding that we do not face challenges alone. Hebrews 13:6 says, *"So we say with confidence, 'The Lord is my helper; I will not be afraid. What can mere mortals do to me?"* God is always with us, and we are never alone in our battles against fear and doubt. Science has found that people who have a strong social or spiritual support system are more resilient in the face of adversity. This underscores the importance of trusting in God's presence and seeking His help in times of fear. When we remind ourselves that God is our helper, we can confidently stand against the forces of fear and doubt.

Finally, the key to overcoming fear and doubt lies in the renewal of the mind, which is a recurring theme in scripture. Romans 12:2 says, *"Do not conform to the pattern of this world, but be transformed by the renewing of your mind."* As we align our thoughts with God's truth, we begin to see fear and doubt as lies that must be rejected. Instead, we embrace the power, love, and sound mind that God has given us. When we daily immerse ourselves in scripture, prayer, and worship, we strengthen our faith, which in turn diminishes the hold that fear and doubt have over our lives. This transformation is both a spiritual and neurological process, demonstrating the profound connection between our faith in God and our ability to live in peace and confidence.

## The Doubt Cycle and how to Shake It

One of the most dangerous cycles of doubt that we take ourselves through is self-doubt. The danger of self-doubt will not allow you to believe in your abilities even if the Bible give countless scriptures of how much power He has endowed upon us. The belief that, "I am not enough" permeates the minds of countless individuals because of a failure mindset. Scriptures like, "God will give wisdom to those who ask, but they must believe and not doubt." James 1:5-8 This verse underscores the truth that the wisdom of God is available for all who ask because it is His will that we do not lack in wisdom of what He has given us all individually. When doubt set in, it brings along with it worry, fear, disbelief, and anxiety. All of which has a negative effect on the physical body when carried for a long period of time.

Doubt is a mental state of which the mind remains suspended between two or more contradictory propositions and is uncertain about them. Doubt on an emotion level is indecision between belief and disbelief. It may involve uncertainty, distrust or lack of conviction on certain facts, actions, motives, or decisions.

Scientists and historians of science have taken on the belief that whenever new evidence arises either by experimentation or evidence, it's their duty to tear it down, approach it as only possible but not true. This process of doubt will lead to certainties and better understanding. However, when individuals operate in doubt, there is usually no end in their mind that can lead to a stable and sure answer. Regardless of this process in our own minds, the Bible is filled with scriptures that counterattacks our doubts. Scriptures like Psalm 139:13-14, *"For you have formed my inward parts; you knitted me together in my mother's womb. I praise you for I am fearfully and wonderfully made. Wonderful are your works; my soul knows it very well."* This scripture simply reminds us of our unique and individual creation by God. It also celebrates the beauty and intricacy of our being, encouraging us to embrace our true selves and dispel self-doubt.

We are all filled with doubt at some point in life. However, the main topic of doubt here is the self-doubt and the doubt about God and anything related to His ability and existence. It's safe to say that we do not have all the answers, but it's worth shaking because doubt inevitably leads to fear. All the fears that you have consider where they may have originated from. If you thoroughly think it through, you will find that your fears derived from doubts you allowed to grow over time. Self-doubt can be debilitating and will inevitably keep you stagnating in certain situations. Learning how to become free and shake the hold of doubt in your mind is worth digging deeper to find the remedy.

Scientifically, in the cognitive domain is mediated by the prefrontal cortex. This causes a loss of motivation or concentration, or feelings of indecisiveness, guilt, shame, or worthlessness, this is when depression can set in. When doubt consumes you, it becomes a part of your make-up and infiltrates your thought patterns. This can now become a place you live in your mind.

Spiritually, the most effective cure for self-doubt is to meditate on God's word which supports your abilities in Christ. Practical ways to shake self-doubt:

- Acknowledge your self-doubt: What is not recognized or acknowledged will not be dispelled.
- Practice self-compassion
- Challenge negative inner thoughts
- Set realistic goals
- Surround yourself with positive people
- Avoid comparisons to others
- Seek professional help when necessary
- Focus on building self-confidence by recognizing your strengths
- Reframe from negative self-talk
- Positive Affirmations
- Meditate on scriptures that affirm who you are as opposed to who you imagine you are

## "The Strength Within: Embracing Your Inner Power Through Faith"

Every person has been uniquely created with strength, resilience, and purpose, but sometimes life's challenges cause us to forget the power that lies within. The Bible consistently encourages us to tap into the strength God has provided, reminding us that through Him, we are more than capable of overcoming obstacles. Ephesians 3:20 assures us, *"Now to him who is able to do immeasurably more than all we ask or imagine, according to his power that is at work within us."* This verse speaks to immeasurable power that resides in each believer, not of our own doing, but through the strength of God working in us. Embracing this inner power begins with understanding that we are never alone, God's presence is with us, equipping us for every battle.

Faith is a catalyst for tapping into this inner strength. Research in psychology shows that individuals who have a strong sense of purpose and believe in something greater than themselves, such as faith in God, experience higher levels of resilience, motivation, and emotional well-being. Faith doesn't merely give us hope; it enables us to push through adversity with a mindset that is grounded in trust and perseverance. Hebrews 11:1 tells us, *"Now faith is confidence in what we hope for and assurance about what we do not see."* When we cultivate a faith that looks beyond our immediate circumstances, we activate the spiritual power within us to face challenges with courage and resilience.

To access your inner strength, it's important to embrace God's promises and recognize His sovereignty over every situation. Strength doesn't always look like physical power or external success, it often manifests as the ability to endure, to stand firm, and to maintain peace even in the midst of trials. The Apostle Paul exemplified this when he wrote in 2 Corinthians 12:9, "But he said to me, *"My grace is sufficient for you, for my power is made perfect in weakness."* When we surrender our weaknesses to God, we make room for His strength to be revealed in our lives. It's in our moment of vulnerability that God's power shines brightest, reminding us that true strength is found in dependence on Him.

Scientific research also supports the concept of embracing your inner strength, demonstrating that belief in one's own capabilities and a sense of purpose can lead to significant psychological and physiological benefits. Studies in positive psychology show that individuals who have a strong sense of self-efficacy, the belief that they can influence outcomes in their lives, tend to exhibit greater resilience and are better able to handle stress. For instance, a study published in the Journal of Personality and Social Psychology found that people with higher levels of self-efficacy experience lower levels of anxiety and depression when facing challenging situations. Additionally, brain research indicates that positive beliefs activate areas of the brain associated with motivation, decision-making, and emotional regulation, strengthening the individual's ability to cope with adversity. This aligns with the biblical understanding of inner strength, where faith in God and the power He has placed within us fuels our capacity, further proving the profound impact that our mindset and faith have on our well-being.

Another key to embracing your inner power is developing resilience through spiritual practices like prayer, meditation on the Word, and worship. These practices are not only a way to connect with God but also have been shown to reduce stress, improve mental clarity, and increase emotional endurance. Philippians 4:6-7 encourages us, "Do not be anxious about anything, but in every situation, by prayer and petition, with thanksgiving, present your requests to God, which transcends all understanding, will guard your hearts and your minds in Christ Jesus." Prayer and worship help center our thoughts on God's truth, providing peace that surpasses the understanding of our circumstances and enabling us to move forward with strength and confidence.

Finally, embracing your inner power through faith involves a mindset shift, one that moves from focusing on limitations to focusing on possibilities. When we align our mindset with God's promises, we recognize that no challenge is too great when we trust in His power working within us. Jesus said in Matthew 17:20, "If you have faith as small as a mustard seed, you can say to this mountain, 'Move from here to there,' and it will move. Nothing will be impossible for you." This is a call to embrace the power of faith, however small, to overcome seemingly insurmountable obstacles. When we remember that our strength comes from God, we are empowered to face life with courage, knowing that His power is at work within us, turning every challenge into an opportunity for growth.

# The Power of Perspective: Shifting Your Mindset for Growth"

Our perspective shapes how we perceive and respond to life's challenges. Science shows that shifting from a fixed mindset, where failure is seen as a limitation, to a growth mindset, where challenges are viewed as opportunities, can significantly improve resilience. Dr. Carol Dweck's research on mindsets reveals that individuals with a growth mindset embrace effort, learn from criticism, and persist in the face of setbacks. This aligns with Romans 12:2, which teaches, "Do not conform to the pattern of this world, but be transformed by the renewing of your mind." Renewing your mind involves intentionally reframing negative thoughts and seeking God's wisdom to view situations through a lens of growth and possibility.

# How to Shift Your Perspective:

### 1. Reframe Challenges as Opportunities

Instead of focusing on the difficulty of a situation, consider what it can teach you. Cognitive-behavioral therapy (CBT) emphasizes the importance of identifying and challenging distorted thoughts. When facing trial, Philippians 4:13 reminds us, "I can do all things through Christ who strengthens me." This verse encourages us to draw on God's strength to turn challenges into steppingstones toward personal and spiritual growth.

### 2. Practice Gratitude Daily

Gratitude shifts the focus from what is lacking to what is abundant. Neuroscience studies show that practicing gratitude activates the brain's reward system, releasing dopamine and serotonin, which promote feelings of happiness and resilience.

Psalm 100:4 encourages us to "Enter his gates with thanksgiving and his courts with praise." Keeping a gratitude journal or expressing thanks to others can train your mind to see blessings even in difficult times.

**3. Seek God's Perspective Through Prayer and Scripture**
Spending time in prayer and meditation on scripture can transform how you view your circumstances. Studies show that prayer reduces stress and strengthens emotional regulation by calming the amygdala and activating the prefrontal cortex. Isaiah 55:8-9 reminds us, "For my thoughts are not your thoughts, neither are your ways my ways." By seeking God's perspective, you align your thoughts with His, finding peace and hope in situations that seem overwhelming.

Shifting your mindset takes intentionality and faith. By reframing challenges, practice gratitude, and seeking God's perspective, you can renew your spirit and build resilience that carries you through life's toughest moments.

**"Resilience grows when faith replaced fear and doubt with strength"**

— Naomi

# Closing Prayer

Heavenly Father,

I come before You, acknowledging the challenges I face and the strength I need to overcome them. Thank you for creating my mind with the ability to grow, adapt, and renew. Lord, I ask that You help me shift my perspective, seeing every obstacle as an opportunity to draw closer to You and grow in wisdom.

Renew my spirit with Your truth, as You promised in Isaiah 40:31, so that I may soar on wings like eagles, run without growing weary, and walk without fainting. Help me to guard my heart and mind, as Proverbs 4:23 teaches, keeping my focus on things that are pure, noble, and praiseworthy.

Lord, give me the strength to reframe my challenges, the gratitude to see Your blessings in every moment, and the humility to seek Your perspective through prayer and scripture. Help me to trust in Your plan, even when the path seems uncertain. Fill me with Your peace and empower me to rise above fear, knowing that through You, I can do all things.

In Jesus' name

Amen.

# Chapter Nine

## Rooted in Truth: Building a Lasting Foundation of Strength through Scripture along with Science

*"Therefore, everyone who hears these words of mine and puts them into practice is like a wise man who built his house on the rock. The rain came down, the streams rose, and the winds blew and beat against the house; yet it did not fall, because it had its foundation on the rock."* *(Matthew 7:24-25) NIV*

In a world of uncertainty and shifting values, building a strong foundation for your life is essential. Rooted in truth, both from God's Word and the discoveries of science, we can cultivate resilience, stability, and purpose. This chapter explores how Scripture and science intersect to provide a lasting framework for strength.

The interplay between scripture and science provides us with a powerful toolkit for understanding our place in the world and building life rooted in truth. We will also explore how biblical principles, and scientific discoveries can work together to create a lasting foundation of mental, emotional, and spiritual strength. By combining timeless truths with modern understanding, we gain clarity, resilience, and purpose.

Building a lasting foundation of strength requires more than just willpower; it requires grounding ourselves in truth, both through scientific understanding and biblical wisdom, biblical wisdom being the principal thing. Science has shown that developing mental resilience and strength begins with a solid foundation of emotional regulation, and a sense of purpose. Research in neuroplasticity indicates that the brain can rewire itself based on repeated thoughts and behaviors, emphasizing the importance of cultivating positive, empowering habits. Similarly, scripture offers a strong foundation lasting strength, urging believers to trust in God's promises and live according to His truth. As Psalm 1:3 describes, *"That person is like a tree planted by streams of water, which yields its fruit in season and whose leaf does not wither, whatever they do prospers."* By rooting ourselves in God's Word, we not only strengthen our spiritual foundation but also set ourselves up for resilience in all aspects of life. The combination of scientific insights and biblical truths creates a comprehensive approach to building lasting strength that withstands the tests of time and adversity.

## The Power of a Firm Foundation

A strong foundation determines the stability of any structure. Jesus used this metaphor in Matthew 7:24:25, saying, *"Therefore, everyone who hears these words of mine and puts them into practice is like a wise man who built his house on the rock. The rain came down, the streams rose, and the winds blew and beat against the house; yet it did not fall, because it had its foundation on the rock."* (Matthew 7:24-25) NIV

*This teaching underscores the importance of grounding our lives in truth. When storms come, be it challenges, doubts, or societal pressures, a life rooted in the truth stands firm. But how do we lay such a*

*foundation? By integrating Scripture's timeless wisdom with the insights of science.*


## Scripture: The Bedrock of Truth


The Bible provides unchanging principles that guide us through every aspect of life. Truth, as revealed in God's Word, anchors us in a world where opinions often fluctuate. Isaiah 40:8 reminds us, *"The grass withers and the flowers fall, but the word of God ensures forever."*

Scripture not only provides moral guidance but also speaks to our identity and purpose. For instance:

- **Jeremiah 29:11**assures us the God has plans for our future, fostering hope and resilience amid uncertainty.
- **Psalm 139:14**declares, "I praise you because I am fearfully and wonderfully made." This truth aligns with the scientific understanding of our intricate biology.

When you immerse yourself in God's Word, it transforms your thinking and builds spiritual strength, and renews your mind as Ephesians 4:23 says, "Be renewed in the spirit of your mind". This verse is part of a passage encouraging believers to leave behind their old ways and embrace a transformed, Christ-centered mindset.


## Science: Affirming the Truth


While Scripture provides the spiritual foundation, science often affirms these truths through observable evidence. Consider the connection between gratitude, a biblical principle, and neuroscience. The

Bible commands us to give thanks in all circumstances (1Thessalonians 5:18), and scientific research shows that practicing gratitude rewires the brain, enhancing mental health and resilience.

## Neuroplasticity: Renewing Your Mind

Science reveals that our brains have the ability to change through neuroplasticity. This aligns with biblical teachings about renewing our minds. Dr. Caroline Leaf, cognitive neuroscientist and Christian author, explains that intentional thought patterns can reshape neural pathways, improving emotional and spiritual well-being.

When Paul encourages believers to "take captive every thought to make it obedient to Christ" (2 Corinthians10:5), he describes a process that science supports. Replacing toxic thought patterns with truth leads to lasting transformation, both spiritually and neurologically.

## Anchoring in Truth: The Role of Scripture and Science

To build a lasting foundation of strength, we must:

**1. Discover the Truth**
Begin with Scripture as your ultimate source of truth. Psalm 119:105 declares, *"Your word is a lamp for my feet, a light on my path."* God's Word illuminates the way, offering clarity and wisdom.

Simultaneously, embraces scientific discoveries that align with and affirm biblical principles. For example, studies on the impact of meditation resonate with the Bible's call to meditate on God's Word day and night **(Joshua 1:8).**

## 2. Apply the Truth

Knowledge alone is insufficient; we must put truth into practice. Neuroscience shows that consistent action strengthens neural connections, creating habits that shape our lives. Likewise, James 1:22 urges us to *"not merely listen to the word, and so deceive yourselves. Do what it says."*

## 3. Build Resilience Through Truth

Resilience is the ability to bounce back from adversity. Research indicates that resilience is strengthened through community, gratitude, and purpose, all themes rooted in scripture. Hebrews 10:24-25 emphasizes the importance of fellowship: *"And let us consider how we may spur one another on toward love and good deeds, not giving up meeting together."*

# The Harmony of Faith and Science

Some may view faith and science as opposing forces, but they complement each other beautifully. Science often reveals the intricacies of God's creation, inspiring awe and deepening faith. As Psalm 19:1 proclaims, *"The heavens declare the glory of God; the skies proclaim the work of his hands."*

Here are a few examples of this harmony:

- **The Universe's Fine-Tuning:** The precision of physical constants, such as gravity, points to intelligent design.
- **Human Biology:** The complexity of DNA mirrors the psalmist's declaration that we are "fearfully and wonderfully made" (**Psalm 139:14**). In Hebrew, the word "fearfully" original translation is "yare" conveys a sense of awe, reverence, and wonder. It reflects the feeling of being

overwhelmed by something so magnificent and beyond human comprehension. It acknowledges that each person is a masterpiece of divine craftsmanship, deserving awe and respect. It reminds us of the sacred value of life and the depth of God's wisdom and power. This reverence for God's creative process calls us to honor Him as Creator and see ourselves and others as intricately and divinely designed.

- **Mental Health:**Practices like gratitude, mindfulness, and forgiveness, encouraged by scripture, are now widely recognized as beneficial by psychologists.

Faith and science are not at odds: instead, they work together to reveal God's truth and glory.

## Practical Steps to Root Yourself in Truth

### 1. Daily Scripture Reading
Start your day with God's Word, allowing it to shape your thoughts and actions. Use apps, devotionals, or study plans to stay consistent.

### 2. Practice Gratitude
Keep a gratitude journal, listing daily blessings. This practice, rooted in scripture (Colossians 3:15), is also scientifically proven to improve mental well-being.

### 3. Meditate on God's Word
Use biblical meditation techniques, such as repeating a verse throughout the day. This aligns with the science of mindfulness, which enhances focus and reduces stress.

### 4. Stay Connected to Community

Surround yourself with people who encourage and challenge you in faith. Community provides emotional support and accountability, fostering resilience.

**5. Seek Knowledge with Discernment**
Explore scientific discoveries with a discerning mind, recognizing that truth ultimately reflects God's design.

## A Life Built on Truth

When we root our lives in the truth of scripture and enrich our understanding through science, we create a foundation that can withstand any storm. As we grow in faith and knowledge, we fulfill the call of Colossians 2:7: *"Rooted and built up in him, strengthened in the faith as you were taught, and overflowing with thankfulness."*

By integrating spiritual and scientific truths, we not only build resilience but also become lights in a world searching for answers. Stay rooted, stay anchored, and let the unchanging truth of God guide your life.

This approach invites you to embrace both faith and reason, standing firm in a world of uncertainty. With scripture as your foundation and science as a tool for deeper understanding, you can build a life of strength, purpose, and lasting impact.

**"A strong foundation in truth, grounded in scripture and supported by science, renews your mind and transforms your life."**

— Naomi

## Closing Prayer

Heavenly Father,

Thank you for being the unshakable foundation upon which we can build our lives. As we seek to align our minds with Your truth, open our hearts to the wisdom of scripture and the insights You've revealed through science. Help us to discern truth, reject negativity, and renew our minds daily. Strengthen us with Your Word so that we may stand firm in every season and grow deeper in faith and understanding. May our lives reflect Your glory as we build on the solid rock of Your promises.

In Jesus' name,

Amen.

# Chapter Ten

## Mind Over Matter: Understanding the Brain and Mind Through Scripture and Science:



In exploring the connection between the brain and the mind, we find that both scripture and science offer profound insights. While the brain is the physical organ within the body, the mind is non-physical, involving thoughts, emotions, and consciousness. Together, they form a complex relationship where the mind influences the brain and vice versa. Understanding these differences is essential for spiritual growth, mental renewal, and physical well-being.

Hebrews 11:3 makes a profound declaration, "By faith the visible world was created by God's word (something unseen – Creatio ex nihilo), demonstrating that the things we can perceive with our senses originated from something beyond our physical realm, or that which is physical was made by that which is nonphysical.

# 1. The Brain and Mind: Physical vs. Non-Physical

Scripture and science both affirm the existence of the physical and non-physical aspects of humanity. The brain is tangible, composed of neurons, synapses, and chemical signals, while the mind is intangible, encompassing thoughts, emotions, and spiritual awareness.

## The Brain: The Physical Organ

The brain is a biological structure responsible for regulating bodily functions, processing sensory information, and storing memories. Neuroscientists describe it as the control center of the body. Key facts about the brain include:

- It contains approximately 86 billion neurons.
- Neural connections, known as synapses, facilitate communication between different regions of the brain.
- The brain operates through electrical and chemical signals, which influence thoughts, emotions, and actions.

## The Mind: The Non-Physical Essence

The mind, in contrast, is non-material and encompasses consciousness, reasoning, and imagination. Scripture often refers to the mind as the seat of thoughts and spiritual understanding. For example, Proverbs 23:7 states, *"For as he thinks in his heart, so is he."* This verse reflects the biblical perspective that our thoughts (mind) shape our identity and behavior.

Dr. Caroline Leaf explains that the mind is the source of thoughts, and these thoughts physically shape the brain. She further explains that toxic thoughts, such as stress, worry, fear, anger and unforgiveness cause damage to the brain. Chemicals are released into the brain, causing chaos and damage. Those toxic thoughts can cause a loss of sleep or of the ability to do your job right, physical illness and more.

In a spiritual sense, these thoughts connect you to the curse. Connecting to the negative thoughts that spring up can destroy the good plan that God has for us. Continuing with the thoughts that do not serve us well will ultimately destroy us. Mark 7:21-22 makes it clear how the negative thoughts can create havoc in our lives if we allow them to take root and become a regular pattern in our lives, *"For from within, out of the heart of man, come evil thoughts, sexual immorality, theft, murder, adultery, coveting, wickedness, deceit, sensuality, envy, slander, pride, foolishness."* This is why it's crucial to take every thought captive and cast down anything that opposes God's truth without delay.

## 2. The Mind Shapes the Brain: Thoughts Lead to Physical Changes

One of the most fascinating aspects of the mind-brain relationship is the ability of the mind to influence the brain physically. This process again is supported by the concept of neuroplasticity, which is the brain's ability to reorganize itself by forming new neural connections based on thoughts and experiences.

**Neuroplasticity: Science Supports Scripture**

Science reveals that repeated thoughts and behaviors create pathways in the brain. For example:

- Positive, intentional thoughts strengthen healthy neural connections.
- Negative, repetitive thinking reinforces destructive patterns.

When negative and repetitive destructive thought patterns form in the brain, they have a profound impact on the body, as the brain's functions are directly tied to physical health. Here's how these patterns affect the body:

- Stress Responses Activation – Negative thoughts trigger the amygdala, the brain's fear center, which activates the stress response system (the hypothalamic-pituitary-adrenal axis, or HPA axis). This results in the release of stress hormones like cortisol and adrenaline.

**Effects on the Body**

- **Increased heart rate**and blood pressure
- **Suppressed immune function,**making the body more susceptive to illness.
- **Digestive issues**such as nausea, cramping, or irritable bowel syndrome (IBS)
- **Chronic stress**from repetitive negative thoughts can lead to conditions like hypertension and heart disease.

## Neural Pathway Reinforcement

Negative thinking creates and strengthens neural pathways associated with stress and fear. Over time, these pathways become dominant, making it harder for the brain to focus on positive thoughts or solutions.

## Effects on the Body

- **Chronic fatigue**due to overactivation of the nervous system.
- **Sleep disturbances,**as the mind struggles to relax.
- **Muscle tension**often leads to headaches, back pain, or joint discomfort.

## Inflammation and Cellular Damage

Prolonged negative thinking can increase inflammatory markers in the body, such as cytokines, which are associated with chronic diseases.

## Effects on the Body

- Increased risk of conditions like diabetes, arthritis, and autoimmune disorders.
- Accelerated cellular aging due to oxidative stress.

## Mental Health Impacts with Physical Consequences

Repetitive negative thought patterns contribute to mental health issues such as depression and anxiety, which further exacerbate physical symptoms.

## Effects on the Body

- **Appetite changes**can lead to weight gain or loss.
- **Chronic pain syndromes**, including fibromyalgia.
- **Weakened immunity,**leaving the body vulnerable to infections.

## The Spiritual and Physical Connection

Scripture warns about the dangers of unchecked negative thoughts, highlighting their destructive potential:

- **Proverbs 17:22:**"A cheerful heart is good medicine, but a crushed spirit dries up the bones."
- **2 Corinthians 10:5:**"We demolish arguments and every pretension that sets itself up against the knowledge of God, and we take captive every thought to make it obedient to Christ."

These verses emphasize the importance of maintaining a healthy mind not only for spiritual health but also for the body's well-being.

Negative and repetitive destructive thoughts don't just harm the mind, they also profoundly impact the body by triggering stress, reinforcing unhealthy neural pathways, and contributing to physical ailments. Breaking this cycle through practices like renewing the mind with scripture, practicing gratitude, and focusing on positive, faith-filled thoughts can lead to both spiritual and physical healing. Philippians 4:8 encourages believers to focus on what is true, noble, and praiseworthy. Doing so not only shapes spiritual well-being but also fosters positive physical changes in the brain.

### How Thoughts Affect the Brain

When the mind processes a thought, whether positive or negative, it triggers chemical and electrical responses in the brain. Over time, these responses shape the brain's structure and function. This interplay underscores the importance of renewing the mind with God's truth to cultivate both spiritual and physical wellness.

## 3. The Spiritual Dimension: The Mind's Role in Connecting with God

The Bible highlights the mind as the space where spiritual battles occur and where transformation begins. The mind is essential for understanding God's Word, discerning truth, and aligning with His will.

### The Battle of the Mind

The apostle Paul describes the struggle between the mind set on the flesh and the mind governed by the Spirit in Romans 8:6: "The mind governed by the flesh is death, but the mind governed by the Spirit is life and peace." This verse emphasizes the mind's spiritual nature and its influence on our overall well-being.

When the mind focuses on God's Word, it aligns with truth, leading to spiritual renewal and physical benefits. Conversely, when the mind dwells on fear, doubt, or sin, it negatively impacts the spirit and body.

**Meditation and Prayer: Bridging Mind and Spirit**

Scripture encourages meditation on God's Word, which strengthens the mind's connection to Him. **Joshua 1:8** says, "Keep this Book of the Law always on your lips; meditate on it day and night."

Science supports this practice, showing that meditation and prayer:

- Reduce stress and anxiety.
- Enhance focus and emotional stability.
- Improve neuroplasticity by reinforcing positive thought patterns

Through meditation on scripture and prayer, the mind becomes a tool for spiritual growth and transformation, influencing the brain's physical structure.

## 4. Toxic Thoughts and Brain Health: Breaking the Cycle

When the mind harbors toxic thoughts, such as fear, anger, and bitterness, it affects the brain's physical health and overall function. This connection highlights the need to address mental and spiritual health together.

**The Science of Toxic Thinking**

Negative thoughts activate the brain's stress response, releasing hormones like cortisol. Prolonged exposure to stress damages neural pathways, shrinking areas like the hippocampus (responsible for memory) and impairing cognitive function.

Biblical Solutions for Toxic Thoughts

Scripture provides practiced steps for breaking free from harmful thought patterns:

**1. Renew Your Mind:**
Romans 12:2 reminds us to be transformed by renewing our minds. This involves replacing toxic thoughts with God's truth.

**2. Guard Your Heart and Mind:**
Proverbs 4:23 says, "Above all else, guard your heart, for everything you do flows from it." Protecting your mind from negativity is essential for spiritual and physical health.

**3. Choose Gratitude:**
Gratitude, as encouraged in 1 Thessalonians 5:18, shifts focus away from negativity and fosters mental and physical healing. Studies show that gratitude rewires the brain, increasing overall happiness and resilience.

# 5. Bridging Faith and Science for Complete Wellness

The harmony between scripture and science reveals that both disciplines point to the same truth: the mind and brain are intricately connected, and both need care.

## Practical Steps for a Healthy Mind and Brain

### 1. Immerse Yourself in God's Word

Reading and meditating on scripture daily transforms the mind and fosters positive neural changes.

### 2. Practice Mindfulness in Prayer

Set aside time to pray and reflect, calming your mind and reducing stress. This aligns with both biblical teaching and scientific findings on mental clarity.

### 3. Cultivate Healthy Thought Patterns

Identify and replace negative thoughts with God's promises. Use scriptures like Jeremiah 29:11 "For I know the plans I have for you," declares the Lord, to shift your focus.

### 4. Engage in Gratitude and Worship

Gratitude and worship improve mental health by fostering a positive mindset and enhancing brain function.

### 5. Seek Community Support

Surround yourself with fellow believers who encourage and challenge you. Community strengthens the mind's resilience and provides accountability.

## The Ultimate Goal: Transformation

The ultimate goal of understanding the brain and mind is transformation, spiritual mental, and physical. As Colossians 3:2 says, "Set your minds on things above, not on earthly things." By aligning our minds with God's truth, we allow His Spirit to renew us from the inside out, influencing our brain, body, and soul.

Understanding the distinction between the brain and the mind is crucial for complete wellness. The mind, as the non-physical seat of thoughts and spiritual awareness, influences the brain's physical structure and function. Scripture and science both affirm the profound connection between the two, emphasizing the importance of cultivating healthy thought patterns and aligning our minds with God's truth.

By renewing the mind through scripture, prayer, and gratitude, we actively shape the brain, fostering resilience and spiritual growth. As we embrace this harmony between faith and science, we fulfill the biblical call to love God with all our heart, soul, and mind (Matthew 22:37) and experience transformation that impacts every aspect of our lives.

## CONCLUSION: Rewired by the Creator

As we come to the end of this journey through the intricate relationship between science and scripture, one truth stands above all: both have the same Author, the same Creator, and the same Originator, God. The Word of God and the discoveries of science are not at odds; rather, they beautifully complement one another, revealing His wisdom, creativity, and purpose for humanity.

Science, with its exploration of the brain's complexity and the mind's capacity for transformation, illuminates the incredible design of the human body, scripture, with its timeless truths, provides the spiritual foundation for understanding our purpose and walking in alignment with God's will. Together, they testify to the One who designed us in His image, equipping us with the tools to experience transformation at every level, spirit, mind, and body.

Paul's words in Romans 12:2 resonate as the cornerstone of this transformation: "Do not conform to the pattern of this world but be transformed by the renewing of your mind." This renewing is not a surface level change; it is a total rewiring, a profound shift in how we think, perceive, and respond. It begins with the recognition that God has given us the ability to take every thought captive, reframe destructive patterns, and align our thinking with His truth.

Science affirms this process through the concept of neuroplasticity, which reveals that our brains can be reshaped by our thoughts. Yet, it is the power of God working through His Word and Spirit that makes this transformation enduring and purposeful. When we surrender our minds to Him, He rewires us from the inside out, allowing us to live with clarity, peace, and strength.

Let this journey remind you that your mind is a gift, intricately designed by God to connect with Him and reflect His glory. Whether you are navigating challenges, breaking free from toxic patterns, or striving for growth, remember that transformation is possible. Through intentional renewal, grounded in scripture and supported by the truths of science, you can experience the abundant life God has planned for you.

As you step forward, may you embrace the opportunity to think differently, live intentionally, and be continually rewired by the Creator. In Him, the author of both scripture and science, we find the power to transform our minds and renew our lives.

**"Your mind shapes your brain- scripture and science reveal how thoughts, guided by the Creator, transform your life."**

— Naomi

## Closing Prayer

Heavenly Father,

Thank You for the incredible gift of our minds and the complexity of our brains, designed in Your wisdom and perfection. As we explore the connection between science and scripture, help us to see Your hand in all creation. Grant us understanding to renew our minds and align our thoughts with Your truth. Teach us to overcome challenges, break free from negativity, and walk in the abundant life You've promised. May this journey draw us closer to You and inspire us to use our minds for Your glory.

In Jesus' name, Amen.

# Chapter Eleven

## The Thought Effect: Unlocking the Mind-Body Connection

*For as he thinketh in his heart, so is he. Proverbs 23:7 (NIV)*

## The Power of a Thought

The Bible and science converge on a profound truth: our thoughts are powerful. Proverbs 23:7 states, "For as he thinketh in his heart, so is he." This ancient wisdom is echoed by modern neuroscience, which reveals how our thoughts influence not just our mental state but also our physical health. This chapter explores the intricate relationship between our thoughts, the mind, the brain, and the body, illustrating how a renewed mind leads to a transformed life.

## The Mind and Its Role in the Thought Process

The mind is not the same as the brain, though they are deeply interconnected. The mind encompasses our consciousness, emotions, and will, elements that drive our thoughts and decisions. Scripture underscores the need to guard and renew our minds. Romans 12:2 reminds us, "Do not conform to the pattern of this world, but be transformed by the renewing of your mind."

The mind operates as the interpreter of thoughts, filtering input from our external environment and internal reflections. This process triggers neural pathways in the brain, laying the groundwork for physical and emotional outcomes.

## The Brain: A Physical Powerhouse of Thoughts

Neuroscientists have discovered that the brain is plastic, meaning it can rewire itself in response to thoughts, a concept known as neuroplasticity, as previously mentioned. Dr. Caroline Leaf, a cognitive neuroscientist, highlights that negative thoughts can create "toxic trees" in the brain, neural clusters associated with stress and harm, while positive, faith-filled thoughts foster healthy growth.

When we think, neurons in our brain fire together, forming neural pathways. Repeated thoughts strengthened these pathways, shaping habits and behaviors. This scientific truth aligns with Proverbs 4:23: "Above all else, guard your heart, for everything you do flows from it."

## Scientific Evidence

- **Amygdala Activation:**Negative thoughts often trigger the amygdala, the brain's fear center, releasing stress hormones like cortisol. Chronic negative thinking can lead to inflammation and diseases such as heart disease and diabetes.
- **Prefrontal Cortex Engagement:**Positive thoughts engage the prefrontal cortex, associated with decision-making and rational thinking, improving emotional regulation and physical health.

## The Thought-Body Connection

Thoughts don't just reside in the mind; they manifest in the body. This is supported by the field of psychoneuroimmunology (PNI), which studies the interaction between psychological processes, the nervous system, and the immune system.

## The Stress Response

When a person experiences chronic negative thoughts, the body enters a prolonged state of stress. This activates the hypothalamic-pituitary-adrenal (HPA) axis, flooding the body with cortisol. Over time, this leads to:

- Suppressed immune function
- Increased blood pressure
- Weight gain (especially abdominal fat)

- Accelerated aging

## Healing Through Positive Thinking

Conversely, focusing on positive, faith-filled thoughts releases dopamine and serotonin, the brain's "feel-good" chemicals. This enhances mood, improves heart health, and strengthens the immune system. Philippians 4:8 encourages believers to think on what is true, noble, right, pure, and lovely, a divine prescription for mental and physical well-being. Also, Proverbs 17:22 says, "A cheerful heart is good medicine, but a crushed spirit dries up the bones."Meaning, a person's attitude affects his outlook on life and even his health.

## Scriptural Foundation: Thoughts and Transformation

The Bible is rich with verses that highlight the power of thoughts:

- **2 Corinthians 10:5:**"We take captive every thought to make it obedient to Christ."This verse underscores the importance of controlling our thought life, ensuring it aligns with God's truth.
- **Isaiah 26:3:**"You will keep in perfect peace those whose minds are steadfast because they trust in you." A steadfast mind focused on God's promises fosters peace, both mentally and physically.

# Practical Steps to Unlock the Mind-Body Connection

## 1. Practice Mind Renewal

Renewing the mind involves actively replacing negative thoughts with positive, truth-filled ones. Colossians 3:2 advises, "Set you minds on things above, not on earthly things."

- Application: Start each day with affirmations rooted in Scripture, such as, "I am fearfully and wonderfully made" (Psalm 139:14).

## 2. Harness Gratitude

Scientific studies reveal that gratitude rewires the brain for positivity, increasing resilience and reducing depression.

- **Application:**Keep a gratitude journal, noting three things you are thankful for daily.

## 3. Meditate on Scripture

Biblical meditation aligns the heart and mind with God's word, promoting peace and clarity.

- **Application:**Spend five minutes daily meditating on a single verse, such as Jeremiah 29:11, and visualize its truth. "For I know the plans I have for you," declares the LORD, "plans to prosper you and not to harm you, plans to give you hope and a future.

## 4. Incorporate Deep Breathing

Deep breathing activates the parasympathetic nervous system, calming the body and mind.

- **Application:**Practice slow, intentional breaths while reciting verses like Psalm 46:10: "Be still, and know that I am God."

## Real-Life Testimony

Consider my story, after a divorce from a traumatic situation, I was plagued by anxiety and negative thoughts. I turned to scripture and began focusing more on gratitude, meditation and prayer. Over time, my health improved, and I experienced joy, peace, and a hope for my future that only by the grace and the love of God could have brought me this far. My transformation mirrors the promise of Philippians 4:7; "And the peace of God, which transcends all understanding, will guard your hearts and your minds in Christ Jesus."

## The Scientific and Spiritual Synergy

Science affirms what Scripture has long taught: our thoughts shape our reality. By renewing the mind, we not only improve brain function but also unlock the body's capacity for healing and restoration.

## Key Takeaways

- Negative thoughts harm both the mind and body, but positive, Scripture-aligned thoughts promote healing and growth.

- Through neuroplasticity, the brain can be rewired for a healthier, more faith-filled life.
- Aligning thoughts with God's Word brings peace, purpose, and vitality.

## Conclusion: A Call to Action

The connection between thoughts, the mind, the brain, and the body are undeniable. Proverbs 18:21 declares, "The tongue has the power of life and death." Similarly, our thoughts have the power to bring life or destruction. By embracing the truth of Scripture and applying practical, science-backed strategies, we can unlock the mind-body connection and live the abundant life God intends.

Let this chapter be your invitation to start each day with intentional, life-giving thoughts, transforming your mind, body, and spirit.

**"Thoughts are the architects of reality, bridging the unseen mind to the physical body and shaping the world within and around us."**

— Naomi

## Closing Prayer

Heavenly Father,

Thank You for the gift of the mind, body, and spirit, which You intricately designed in Your wisdom. Your Word reminds me that as I think in my heart, so I am. I ask for Your guidance in renewing my thoughts daily, aligning then with Your truth and promises.

Lord, help me to guard my mind against negativity and fear, replacing them with faith, gratitude, and love. Teach me to meditate on what is true, noble, and praiseworthy so that my mind is transformed, my brain rewired for Your purpose.

I surrender every anxious thought, every doubt, and every fear to You. Replace them with peace that surpasses all understanding. Let the power of Your Holy Spirit guide my thoughts, filling me with joy, healing, and hope.

Father, thank You for revelation that my thoughts can bring life to my body and soul. May I walk in the freedom and victory that comes from setting my mind on things above. Use my renewed mind to reflect Your glory in all I do.

In Jesus's name.

Amen.

Naomi Greenlee